MY TRUCK DRIVING LIFE

with Bonus Classic Car Short Stories

Daniel S Bridger

This book is dedicated to the memory of my mother Agnes Clara Konitzer Bridger Bast. I wish she were still here to thank for her part in this endeavor. She always encouraged her children to read from an early age. Mom spent many years researching our family geneology and was a prolific writer.

I have to also thank my brother Russ for the inspiration to start writing back in 2012. He got me interested in writing a blog back when I started reading his own book publishing blog he created. He successfully published quite a few books written by our mom and other authors, enabling them to leave a written history of their lives and accomplishments.

"Truck driving is the only profession practiced mainly in the field of amateurs"

AUTHOR UNKOWN

"Truck drivers are a 'dime a dozen' but good ones are always hard to find."

JIM BRYE

CONTENTS

PREFACE

Having three brothers and two sisters, it seems odd that all the male siblings eventually decided making driving a career choice. The two girls were never drawn to it. Being the oldest I had been thinking about how and why driving had become such a big part of my own life. I can trace it back to my dad's youngest sibling, Uncle Jim, whom I haven't seen in more than 30 years. He lives on Marathon Island in the Florida Keys and doesn't like to leave paradise, nor the sailboat he lives on, except when a hurricane is forecast.

I'm sure he was partly responsible for a couple of ways my life turned out as far as driving.

My fascination with Corvettes started during my pre-teen years, thanks to Uncle Jim. My dad's brother enlisted and became a US Marine back in the mid 1950's. Four years later, when he got out of the service, he came home and with the cash he had saved up, bought a used 1959 or 60 jet black Corvette convertible with a red interior.

To get up close and touch that car as a youngster was awesome and fueled my lifelong desire to own and drive a Corvette. I have been fortunate to have had the opportunity to own two, a 1967 StingRay and a 1999 C5 model. That was the first influence he had on me.

Read on:

MIKE KAUFFMAN PHOTO

Ryder Integrated Logistics tractor pulling Swire Coca-
Cola trailers based out of Salt Lake City, Utah

THE
1960'S

My First Road Trip

Uncle Jim also took me on my first road trip sometime in the early 1960's when I was 9 or 10 years of age. After being trained in some type of electronics and radio while he was in the Marine Corps, he obtained a good job in Milwaukee, Wi (I think it was General Electric) working in the same field. He had a hand in building some type of computer or electronic equipment that was enclosed in a very large metal cabinet. I was too young to understand what it was all about, but they needed to get it delivered to a university in southern Michigan near Detroit (could have been Lansing or Ann Arbor). It was deemed too valuable and risky to put it on a carrier, so they asked my uncle if he would transport it in a van and make the delivery in person.

Uncle Jim accepted the assignment and asked me if I wanted to go along with him to keep him company on the overnight trip from Milwaukee. I was surprised that he asked me and said "sure". Jim had two sons of his own, but they were much younger than I was, he must have figured that I would have gained a greater appreciation of the experience. On the bright summer day we were to leave he drove up in front of the house with a big white panel van with this huge cabinet full of electronics taking up the entire cargo area. We were living at 19th and Chambers St. in Milwaukee at the time. He came into the house and announced that there was only one seat for the driver and we would have to figure something out. He eyed a step stool that we had in the pantry and took it out to the van, that was my chair for the next two days!

Well, it wasn't very comfortable but I had a fascinating trip with him. I remember going through Chicago for the first time, such a huge city with so many cars and trucks. I wondered how he could drive through it and not get lost. We drove around Lake Michigan and east on I-94 towards Detroit.

As we got into the early evening Uncle Jim decided to call it a day and we pulled into a Holiday Inn (or a Howard Johnson's) to check in and get a room. I had never stayed in a motel before in my life. After getting our room, it was time to get some dinner, so he took me to the restaurant at the hotel which seemed to be really fancy and high class to me. My family almost never ate in restaurants. Money was tight in our household and the occasional splurge for us was bringing home George Webb hamburgers (7 for a buck, with Green Sheet coupon!) or mom making a Chef Boyardee pizza. There were only a couple McDonald's drive-ins in Milwaukee back then and I don't think we had even tried them yet.

My eyeballs must have been bulging as a waiter handed me this huge menu to look at. I asked my uncle what to do and he said I could have anything I wanted on the menu! His expenses were being covered by his company and he didn't care what I had. I was stunned and don't remember what I ended up eating, but I'm sure it was good.

The next morning we got up and continued on. As we drove through Battle Creek, I remember him telling me that was the home of Kellogg's, where they made all the breakfast cereal. We continued on and arrived a while later at the university where my uncle went in with the paperwork. He backed up to a garage door and 3 or 4 big burly guys came out and carried the cabinet inside. Then we turned around and headed home.

I'm sure the fond memories of that road trip with Uncle Jim helped me to consider driving as a career in my later years. It's funny how childhood experiences can influence the direction you take in life. Truck driving is not an easy life, I was fortunate to have worked for two good companies nearly all of my trucking career, made decent money and was able to somewhat indulge my passion for cars, owning a few great ones.

THE
1970'S

Throughout the 1970's I was a franchised gasoline station dealer with an ice making business on the side living in Milwaukee, Wisconsin. Growing tired of living in the big city, I wanted to follow my buddy and his wife whom had moved to the small northern Wisconsin town of Crivitz in 1979. I was spending all of my free time and week-ends driving back and forth. My problem was, what would I do about employment? There were not a lot of well paying jobs in that rural area. The oil company (Clark Oil & Refining) I had a franchise with was trying to force out us dealers and replace them with salaried managers at every location they could gain control of. Seeing the "writing on the wall", I decided that a career change was in order.

Schwerman Trucking would come to my station delivering gasoline in their semi-tanker trucks every week or so. One driver had a fancy Peterbuilt tractor and I remember standing outside the cab looking at all the dashboard switches and gauges in amazement. To me, it looked like an airplane cockpit and got me thinking about trucking as an option. In the Army Reserve, I was trained as a truck driver (up to 5 ton) and decided I would look for a school to get trained and qualified on the big rigs.

THE 1980'S

The school I chose was the Diesel Truck Driving School in Sun Prairie, Wisconsin and turned out to be a good choice. That was in 1980. They have been in business since 1963 and still operate today, not only training truck drivers, but crane operators as well. I will never forget one of the trainers named Red (older, kind of moody guy). He would be in the passenger seat as you were driving and whack you on the shoulder when you did something wrong. Scared the heck out of me, but he was effective! I've been tempted to whack a few of the guys I've had to train over the years, never did it though!

I spent seven week-ends at the school about 90 miles west of Milwaukee. Classes lasted 12 hours per day on Saturdays and Sundays, so I had to get a motel near the school on those week-ends. After graduating at the top of my class of 29, I set out to find someone to drive for, which was not easy. My initial goal was to look for a company near Crivitz, where I wanted to relocate, but that was not to be, as there were very few opportunities for a rookie driver in that rural area.

While back in Milwaukee I started knocking on a lot of doors and filling out numerous applications. Finally, after a few months, my best friend Bob and his wife Mary tipped me off to a small cartage company with a driver that had just resigned. I think the guy that quit was a nephew of Mary. After filling out an application and interviewing with the owner, he decided to give me a chance. To this day I wonder if he was testing me, as he assigned me an old Consolidated Freightways half cab cab-over that had just been painted. Problem was, they had removed the side windows for painting and no one had put them back in! I was told," we'll get those windows in as soon as we can". As I did not know how to install them myself, I drove that tractor for two weeks in September, Wisconsin weather without windows! I was freezing my ass off, but I didn't complain. The mechanic finally took pity on me and put the windows back in! After having been there only about 6 months, the owner bought the first brand new tractor he had ever purchased. Upon hearing a few senior drivers belly ache about it being a day cab, he assigned that brand new tractor to me! Man, was I proud, but I'm sure it ticked off many of the other drivers! But, even being the newbie, I had a pretty good relationship with most of them.

As most all of you veteran drivers know out there, you have to pay your dues and gain safe driving experience before you can land a good job. I spent a year hauling piggy-back containers back and forth from the rail yard and Port of Milwaukee ship piers to customers. The job was based on 25% of gross and there was not much money to be made. Everyone has to start somewhere and I will always be grateful to owner Jeff Long of Harry H Long Moving, Storage & Express and Montana Trucking. As far as I know they are still going at 960 W. Montana Ave in Milwaukee. I safely completed my first year (1980 to 1981) with no accidents, but one very close call.

Close Call

One afternoon, three of us drivers got dispatched at the same time to pick up container loads at the rail-yard to deliver the following day. We each had a chassis with empty 20 foot containers to take back and turn in. I followed a driver out with the other behind me as we proceeded through the city to the yard. As we approached a big intersection the driver in front of me went though turning left. As I approached, the light went yellow and I speeded up into the turn thinking the guy behind me may want to get through.

Containers on chassis have a very high center of gravity and you have to be careful with turns. As I went through the driver behind me saw the left side trailer tires come completely off the ground and I very nearly tipped the tractor-trailer over. One careless action and I almost paid the price. Since I was in my first year of professional driving, that could have been a very early end of my new career. I learned a lesson and my trucking journey was able to continue!

My first driving job lasted from Sept, 1980 to Sept, 1981. I wasn't making a lot of money, thankfully I still had the gas station to supplement my income. I was able to partner with my buddy's brother, who managed the station for me while he was still in college. I was still trying to relocate and every chance I could get away, would be up north knocking on doors and filling out applications.

By sheer coincidence, I was up there one week-end and received a tip that two drivers from the Frigo Cheese company were fired very recently. Well, I extended my week-end into Monday and drove down to Lena (20 miles away) first thing in the morning. I filled out an application and was told I would be contacted, if they were interested. I had listed my friend's address and phone number as my address on the application. I then drove 20 miles back to Bob's house, wasn't there more than a half hour and the transportation manager called, asking when I could come for an interview. After telling him I could be back in 20 minutes, he laughed and said that the following day would be fine.

The next day I went down, interviewed and was hired as a local driver out of the Crivitz plant. And that is how I was able to make the move to "up north".

Living in Crivitz

Frigo Cheese had a Crivitz packaging plant 20 miles from the main plant in Lena and a primary part of my job was running truckloads of cheese down to Lena and supplies back. I was paid by the hour and sometimes it was hard to get a full 40 hour week. After a year and a half of running local, I made one of the worst decisions of my life, leaving the Frigo Cheese Corp!

I had the itch to get on the road and see the country (also to make some good money). There were no over the road positions available with Frigo, so I decided to go to another company called Bird Trucking out of Waupun, Wisconsin.

They were trying to compete with Schneider National and steal as much business from them as they could. It turned out to be a disaster for me as they were paying a percentage of the load and empty miles were not compensated at all. I quickly learned what it was like to work for next to nothing after road expenses and knew that I had made a bad mistake. I lasted three months with Bird.

The breaking point for me came after I had spent half a day unloading (for a $10.00 stop pay), another half a day (no pay) waiting for the next dispatch. Back in those days, it was before the cell phone era. Waiting a half day for a load consisted of parking in a truck stop and walking in to a pay phone and calling dispatch every hour. Standard dispatcher response: "nothing yet, call me in an hour"! Then they wanted me to spend most of the night deadheading 400 miles to pick up a return load (once again, no pay and no real rest)! If you add it all up, that is being away from home in a truck for almost a full day making $10.00! I refused the load and was told to bring the truck home.

Thankfully I already had another job lined up with a different company. By the way, Bird Trucking did not last very long, as they went belly up not long after.

Railroad Crossing Lesson

Sometimes, you learn the hard way. In more 37 years of professional driving, I have gotten three citations in a truck, two for speed and one for an illegal turn.

The one for the turn came as a result of not paying attention at a rail crossing in 1983 while with Bird Trucking. Having been driving professionally for only a couple years, I was in rural South Carolina and made a wrong turn. In an effort to get "squared away", I saw a large empty lot off to the left at a cross street. There was a railroad track running parallel to the highway in the median of a divided road, and in my hurry to get turned around, totally missed seeing the no left turn sign. On top of that, I didn't notice how high the grade was that the track was on! Proceeding into the turn across the tracks, I heard the landing gear of the trailer skidding on the pavement and went hard to the brakes. It was too late and I was high centered across the track! The trailer was loaded and the landing gear raised as high as it could go, I was screwed and there was no way I was getting off that track without help.

Thankfully, there was a little store right there with a payphone (remember those?), so I was able to call the police and get any oncoming trains stopped. Out comes a South Carolina Sheriff's Deputy and he chewed me out before proceeding to write that ticket. He pointed out to me that the reason for the no left turn sign was the high grade of the track. Turned out there were no trains scheduled to come through and a tow truck came out and got me off the track. It was a very embarrassing afternoon! The situation could have been a lot worse though, we all need to be aware at railroad crossings. In 2013, the penalties for FMCSA regulated drivers were increased and are very severe for railroad crossing violations. The fine is $2,750.00 and your CDL will be suspended for 60 days for a first violation. If I remember correctly, my ticket cost me about $60.00, but in 1983, even that wasn't cheap.

After deadheading back to Wisconsin and cleaning out my Bird tractor, the following week I reported for work at my new job. The next three months turned out to be nearly as bad of an experience. I went to work for a pretty decent guy that had about 5 tractors leased on to a refrigerated carrier L.C.L. Transit out of Green Bay, Wi. Thinking that this would be a much better job, he was paying by the mile for "book miles" plus 10%. And I only had to run the midwest and no east coast. Well, I quickly found out that at book plus 10%, I was still being paid for only about 90% of the miles I was running! That and $10.00 per stop at grocery warehouses were a wake up call to me. It was not at all unusual to get jacked around for a half day at a grocery warehouse to get a few pallets off. It didn't take long to see I was not going to be able to make a decent living with this guy either! About three months into that job, the last straw came in Solon, Ohio at the "infamous" company called Stouffer's Foods. Yeah, that one, the frozen food maker that produces French Bread Pizza, Lasagna and hundreds of other items.

Stouffers

In more than 30 years of driving, I have never been treated worse by a company than that day at Stouffer's Foods in the summer of 1983. I was made to feel like their slave, as they treated all drivers. I was assigned to pick up a load at their facility. Being the middle of summer, all I had in the truck was a light jacket. After checking in, I was told to pre-cool my reefer trailer to 0 degrees, which I did. After backing into the dock and waiting, a supervisor came out to the truck, practically screaming that if I didn't get in there to verify "load & count", I would not be loaded.

OK, so now I am standing on the dock with the dock temperature at zero degrees, my trailer pre-cooled to zero degrees and the "loaders" bringing out the "products" from a huge freezer that is kept at 30 below zero. Oh and by the way, the loads are taken off pallets and manually stacked in the trailer floor to ceiling! So, it's zero degrees with a light jacket and I soon discover that if I do not help "stack" the product, the "loaders" disappear for extended periods of time! And me, poor sucker, can't go anywhere because I have to verify load & count whenever they feel like coming back! They would start out with two loaders loading and after you get the hint and start to help, one of them disappears! not to be seen again! It took about 4 to 5 hours to load that trailer and I was never so cold in my life.

I damn near walked off that job right then and there. And as icing on a frozen cake, the load had four stops of floor loaded product that the I had to off load by my lonesome self onto pallets at the grocery warehouses! If I remember correctly, there were over 4 thousand boxes to off load (but I'm sure it was more than 1,000)!

That day scared me, as I had responsibilities at home, a house payment to make and damn near quit a job with no prospects of employment. I will never forget it.

"Every word in the preceding statements about Stouffer's is true to the best of my recollection. They may be a different company now, I certainly hope so, writing this, I am still so angry after all these years."

Since that day in 1983, I have never, ever intentionally bought a Stouffer's product at a grocery store. It's been my personal boycott and will be as long as I live. Many years ago, when still with my ex-wife, I found some Stouffer's French Bread Pizzas in the freezer and we had quite a heated discussion about it. Don't remember what she ended up doing with that stuff, but I refused to eat any of it!

That day in 1983 quickly ended my days hauling L.C.L. Transit Loads. It wasn't long after that, L.C.L. Transit folded up also. Don't know what happened to the guy I worked for. I wish I could remember his name. He was a decent guy with 5 trucks just trying to make a go of it. I did give him proper notice so that he could find another driver. On to the next stage of my career!

I had worked at Frigo Cheese Corp for a year and a half made one the most foolish decisions of my life by quitting. Lasting 3 months with one carrier and 3 months with a second was not the plan! Thought I would be making good money, but I was just getting by and was really disgusted, miserable and never home. So, I made the decision to go back to Frigo Cheese, see the Traffic Manager and ask if he would consider re-hiring me. I figured the worst that could happen was for him to laugh at me and throw me out of his office! After what I had been through, I could handle that. It turned out, he was very tough and grilled me for quite a while. He then sent me on my way, saying that he would have to think about it. I found out later, that he went to the other drivers and asked them if they had any objections to me coming back. Thankfully, I had a good relationship with all of them as well as with the dispatchers. I was allowed to come back and very grateful for the chance!

So from 1983 to 1991 I was a pretty well satisfied company driver. While I was gone those 6 months, Frigo Cheese had closed the Crivitz packaging plant and several others to consolidate production and packaging at the main plant, so I had to work out of Lena. I was making a good living and only had to layover in the truck on average one or two nights a week. We had excellent equipment and I was running within a five state area around Wisconsin and able to make extra money hauling some milk loads on the weekend.

The Anteater

In 1985 news of the revolutionary new aerodynamic Kenworth came out. The traffic manager we had at the time was blown away by the concept and started to research ideas of how he could get these new tractors into our fleet. We were only two years into five year leases on our Freightliner tractors from Penske and you just can't cancel leases with the click of your fingers. He talked to a Kenworth dealer in Green Bay and managed to get a T600 demo tractor to use for a couple of weeks at no charge. We drivers took turns behind the wheel and the consensus was, it was a great tractor with a good ride and plenty of power with the Detroit Series 60 engine. Although very odd looking, almost all the drivers gave it a thumbs up. These tractors were so revolutionary, I remember the stares, honking horns and thumbs-up we would get from 4-wheelers and other trucks going down the highway! I stopped at the house in Crivitz to give my ex-wife a short ride and she made the comment that it looked like I was driving a spaceship!

Our boss then started working numbers with Penske about ordering a new fleet of T600s and turning in our current tractors. The penalty it would cost Frigo was about $50,000 for eight tractors, which was a lot of money in the mid 80's, even for a company the size of Frigo cheese Corp!

After considering the cost, he came up with a brilliant idea that he took to his superiors. By being the first fleet in northern Wisconsin to obtain these new tractors, the value of the publicity, free advertising and exposure for the company would more than offset the costs of breaking our lease! After some serious consideration, the CEO agreed and gave his approval, the tractors were ordered!

It took a couple months to get them in as we all were excitedly waiting. Our traffic manager was a big believer in looking professional and we had some great looking uniforms provided to us after he came onboard. The day we went down to Green Bay to pick the tractors up, our boss had all the local news media there to cover the story as our convoy of eight new 1986 T600s headed back north to Lena. They had camera crews on the overpasses of the freeway to film us as we went by. I'll tell you what, we were some pretty proud drivers, and for many months we enjoyed all the looks and attention from everyone. They must have gotten more than their money's worth with all the publicity, as our traffic manager received a promotion not long after!

So, In the 1980's I was able to buy a decent house, was living in a great rural area and was pretty content. Every deer hunting season, all I had to do was shoot one out in the back yard to fill the freezer. My plan was to retire living in Crivitz and never leave that company. If anyone had told me then that I would spend 25 years living out west in Utah, I would have said they were NUTS!

THE 1990'S

T owards the end of 1990, the winds of change started to blow. That is when I started to learn about 3rd party logistics, the newer, fast growing trend in the trucking industry. There was a lot of competition in the cheese business and Frigo was struggling to keep costs under control. In late '90 & early '91, a corporate decision was made to get out of the transportation business and concentrate their efforts on making cheese. They decided to take bids from Schneider, Penske, Ryder and others to handle their logistics, including providing drivers, logistics managers and tractors to handle the business. Of course that would mean big changes for us company drivers and it wasn't long before we heard the rumors of what was about to happen.

A series of meetings were held with the drivers, dispatchers and the traffic manager exploring ways for us to cut costs, but the eventual final decision from the company was to award a 3 year contract to 3rd party logistics provider, Ryder Integrated Logistics. At the time, the company name was Ryder Dedicated Resources, division of Ryder Systems, Inc. They would provide the tractors and drivers to handle the outbound shipments of Frigo's products and generate back-haul revenue for the company finding freight on the return trips. As you can imagine, this was a life changing event for the drivers and none of them, me included, were happy about it. Before all this transpired, I would have never imagined leaving Frigo. Most of the drivers, I'm sure, were planning to work there until retirement. It was a very hard time for everyone, and we were soon given notice, our employment with Frigo was going to end. Our choice was to either fill out an application with Ryder or seek employment elsewhere. There were about a half dozen drivers that were domiciled in Big Stone City, SD whose jobs were also going to be eliminated. I remember all too well, being called up to the dispatch office one afternoon. One of the South Dakota drivers nearly had a nervous breakdown and I was asked to drive him and his rig back to Big Stone City. It was an awful time. Some drivers left in disgust, others, including me decided to give Ryder a try. I then filled out the application, was interviewed and offered a job. Of course, there were some operational changes that Ryder was going to put in place and one of them was to eliminate one local driver position (I was considered local). Being the lowest in seniority, that meant I had to go over the road.

In November of 1991, my employment with Frigo Cheese ended and a new chapter in my life began with Ryder Integrated Logistics! Needless to say, I was not a happy camper to start with. As mentioned, I was forced to go over the road as Ryder eliminated one local driving position and I had the least seniority at Frigo Cheese. I was certainly not looking forward to it, as the memories of being on the road those 6 months in 1983 came flooding back. I had been running a five state area with occasional single night layovers, and really didn't want to go back to living in a truck.

When Ryder management went over what the new dispatch procedures would be on orientation day, there seemed to be a ray of hope. There would be 9 over the road drivers at our location and each week, the supervisor would choose 9 routes for our drivers. The loads that Ryder didn't take were brokered to outside carriers. The area we covered was basically everything east of the Rockies. Every driver had a seniority number and the first week, driver 1 would choose his load from what was available. Next, driver 2 would choose from the remaining 8 loads and so on down to the last driver who had to take the last available run. The following week, the driver who had the last pick moved to the top of the board and had the first pick of those runs. And so, whoever had first pick, would move down the board weekly until he got to the top again. With this procedure there were only one out of every 9 weeks that we didn't have at least some choice in choosing where we wanted to go.

I started out picking mostly shorter runs that stayed in the Midwest, but quickly found out that I needed to grab the miles on longer runs when I could to make decent money. My original intent was to take the short routes, get home early on Wednesday or Thursday and run some milk loads before having to go out on Sunday again. That didn't work out, as they phased us Ryder drivers out of hauling their milk and all loads went to outside carriers. It wasn't long before I discovered the Texas and Florida loads were always the first to be picked and I would grab them whenever I could. My favorite run would be from Lena to Dallas, then make a triangle to San Antonio and Houston, before coming home. The one great thing with Ryder, they needed to get us home EVERY week, because they needed to reload our trailers and have us ready to go on the following week's loads. There was no sitting around truck stops for a day or two waiting for them to find a back-haul. If they couldn't find anything to bring back within a reasonable amount of time, they would dead-head us home.

Working with this dispatch system, I was doing OK. My Ryder

Logistics Manager was a decent person whom I got along with, as well as our dispatcher. I had a nice Kenworth T600 tractor with a walk-in sleeper, set it up with TV, VCR, cooler, etc and was able to be home enough that my life was not bad. Some of the runs sucked, but some were pretty enjoyable. I had gotten used to my life and didn't have a constant need to "get off the road". For that, I have a lot of thanks for Brad Millikin, our former Logistics Manager. When Ryder first took over, they brought a manager named John up from Chicago. There was some friction between us as I had to become educated in the "Ryder Way". Turned out, after a few months, there was also some friction developing between John and the customer (Frigo Cheese). Suddenly, a change was made and they brought Brad up from Chicago to replace John. Brad fell in love with northern Wisconsin, bought a house in Sobieski (near Green Bay) and moved his wife and kids up. He was a smart guy, easy to get along with and was a pleasure to work for. Although he moved on from Ryder a few years ago, I believe he and his family are still in Wisconsin.

Cheesehead Driver and the
Indiana State Trooper

As previously mentioned, I've gotten three citations (in a tractor trailer) during my trucking career. Two were for speed and one for an illegal U turn (never saw the sign). Unfortunately, one of those citations came as a result of meeting an Indiana State Trooper.

One Sunday afternoon about 1992, I was running south down I-65 in Indiana with a multi-stop load headed for Ohio and West Virginia. Back then, in Indiana and several other states, they had a split speed limit, 65 MPH car and 55 MPH for trucks. Traffic was fairly heavy, but the flow was smooth with everyone cruising at about 65 (of course in the left lane several were driving as fast as they could). Back in those days, radar detectors were not illegal in trucks and I always ran with one. Well, suddenly my detector alerted and I looked over in the oncoming lanes and noticed an unmarked blue high performance IROC Camaro, driven by a trooper. I saw his brake lights come on, but wondered how he would be able nail me with all the traffic I was in.

Sure enough, he came up behind me and put the lights on! I pulled off on the shoulder and waited, observing a "giant" struggling to get out of that small car. He had to put both legs out sideways, both feet on the ground to raise himself up out of that thing. He had to have been at least 6 foot 5 or better. He then reached back in, grabbed his Smokey Bear hat, put it on and came walking up to the tractor. With a big wad of tobacco in his mouth, he asked if I knew how fast I was going and I replied that I wasn't sure and just going with the flow as not to impede traffic. In a very annoyed and loud voice, he replied "Boy!, you ain't s'pose to go with the flow of traffic, you s'pose to be doing 55!" " I'm going to write you up for 65 MPH and do a Level One inspection on you!" Jeeze, I thought, this guy must have swallowed too much of that tobacco juice, what set him off? So I sat there for 45 minutes while he crawled all over that truck and trailer looking for more stuff to write up. What a great afternoon. With the cost of a lawyer, it was more than $500.00 to keep that ticket off my record!

You won't believe the rest of this story, but I swear that it is true. Later that week, on the return trip to Wisconsin, I was on the same interstate. It was Wednesday or Thursday, traffic was light and I was running by myself. I came up over a small rise on the highway and my detector lit up a warning. The same trooper in the same Camaro was sitting in the median and had a dead spot-on reading on my truck! I had my cruise set at 62 MPH and my heart had to have skipped more than a few beats. I looked at him and he was glaring right at me. I must have been within his tolerance, or he just didn't feel like trying to get out of his car, as he let me go by! You can bet your life that every trip through that area afterwards, I was a very good boy!

After about a year and a half with Ryder, early 1993, one of three local drivers resigned. As soon as I found out, I went to the Logistics Manager, requested that job and was given it. I was pretty happy, surviving that time on the road and now able to go back to what I was doing for so many years before Ryder took over. Life was looking very good at that point, although Frigo had been sold to a new owner and rumors were flying.

Winds of Change

And, wouldn't you just know it? The "winds of change" started to blow again! Back in the 1980's, if anyone would have suggested that I would move from Wisconsin and live out west In Utah (for almost 25 years), I would have said they were full of bananas (or honey, but at the time I didn't know that Utah was known as the "beehive" state!). I had never, ever considered the possibility of leaving "Packerland". I was happy in a small town, rural area about 50 miles north of Green Bay. Had a decent house that I could afford with three acres of land, peace and quiet. And I could "hunt" deer in my backyard every hunting season!

I had spent about a year with Ryder up until the end of 1992 and had settled in with them. I wasn't unhappy and was making a decent living. We had been hearing rumors of Frigo Cheese's continuing financial difficulty, but I figured the milk and cheese markets are always up and down and they would weather the then current situation. Suddenly, in early 1993, it was announced that Frigo had been sold to an outside buyer. He would retain the Frigo name and trademarks, but he was the new man in charge.

And the "new man in charge", we soon found out, was not fond of 3rd party logistics providers. Seemed like he was more interested in finding the cheapest "provider" of transportation than in customer service. Although Ryder had a three year contract and Frigo Cheese had a five year obligation on the tractors, he was looking for ways to get out of it, even taking bids from other trucking companies to assume the contract.

I remember coming in off a run one afternoon, parking my tractor to go home, and two men approached me asking for the truck keys. I asked what for and they said they were there to appraise the tractors in order make an offer for the logistics contract. I went upstairs to my boss and asked what the hell was going on and was told to cooperate. That was a fun afternoon.

Looked like "the writing was on the wall" again! One of the great things about Ryder is that if you maintain a good work record, you can transfer anywhere in the country they have an opening. They will always let you transfer before they hire from outside.

So, not knowing what the future held, and after spending a couple months thinking about it, we decided to put our house up for sale. We were almost a year and a half into Ryder's contract and I just could not see the possibility of Frigo renewing. The wife I had at the time had lived in Salt Lake City with her ex-husband for 15 years and always felt it was a good place to live, so I scheduled two weeks vacation in June of 1993 to drive out there and check it out. I wanted to visit the Ryder accounts in Salt Lake City, Las Vegas, and Reno, and see what was available. Our first stop was Salt Lake, where we had an account with Swire Coca-Cola. I stopped by and was introduced to the Senior Operations Manager, Craig. He interrupted a meeting he was in with another person to invite me in and the three of us talked for quite a while. He explained what the job was all about, even though they didn't have any current need for a driver. Craig even took me over for a plant tour, and I was so impressed with him and the operation that I made the decision right then and there, asking to be considered for the next available opportunity to transfer. We then went on our way to Las Vegas and Reno to visit the other Ryder locations. Nothing we saw changed my mind and the second week, we went back to Salt Lake City. It seemed like a nice place to live and I stopped by the Ryder office to let them know that I was still interested in transferring. Michelle was one of the supervisors and when I went in to say hello, she said "Guess what? We had two drivers resign in the past week. When can you be out here?"

Talk about sudden reality! Holy Cow, I had to get on the phone with my manager back in Wisconsin and ask permission to transfer. He said yes, but he wanted two weeks, which was good with me. We then ran around the rest of the day looking for an apartment, found one, and put a deposit down. Then it was a race back to Wisconsin (stopping for gas, food, and to change drivers only) as I had a heck of a lot of planning and packing to do, as well as work two more weeks with Frigo.

On top of all that, I had special ordered a brand new 1993 Camaro Z28 from my Crivitz Chevy dealer and was waiting for them to build and ship it.

The Camaro

One of the great cars I have been fortunate to own was a 1993 Camaro. That was the first model year of the completely redesigned new car. Frankly, the previous generation of the Camaros had lousy reviews and were of poor quality. The assembly lines were so worn out that Chevy resorted to gluing some of the body panels together to cut down on squeaks and rattles.

In 1992 I started reading about a new, redesigned from the ground up model coming out that would use the LT-1 Corvette motor in the high performance Z-28 version. And the Z-28 would cost many thousands less than the Corvette!

Well, after doing a lot of research, it took a few months to convince my wife that we really "needed" this car! Finally, one day I got her into a dealership to look and at least sit in the car. Immediately, she complained that she couldn't see the front of the car and she would be unable to drive it. I finally wore her down. After promising her that I would put something on the front end of the car so she would know where it is, she agreed.

Then, talking to the salesman came my wake up call. We had stopped at a Chevrolet dealer in Green Bay, which was a much bigger city than the small town I was living in. Although our little town of Crivitz had a Chevy dealer, I believed that I could get a better price in the "big" city. We approached a salesman and I asked what kind of a deal he could make me on a new Z-28? His response was something to the effect that they were selling every Camaro that came in. I said "that's fine, I can special order one and wait". He then said they were getting about $2000.00 over "sticker" for them! I said something to the effect that it would be a cold day in hell before I let anyone rip me off like that! We then turned around and headed out the door.

The next day, I went in to see our small town Chevy dealer, the salesman was also a co-owner of the dealership. Knowing that they didn't have any new Camaros in stock, I walked up to him and said hello. I just stated in a matter of fact way that I wanted to buy a new Z-28 Camaro, wanted to patronize a local dealer and was willing to wait to have it built. I then stated that I knew what the invoice pricing to the dealer was and I was willing to give him $900.00 over his invoice. I just about fell over when, without even hesitating, he said "sure"! We went to his office to spec the car and about an hour later we had a deal. Joe Banaszak of Banaszak Chevrolet retired many years ago (the dealership has been sold), but he was a good guy to buy a car from and I'll always be grateful. He actually tried to give me another great deal a few years later on my second Corvette, which unfortunately, he wasn't allowed to do because of GM's quota system!

Indeed, production was behind schedule and I ended up waiting a few months for the car. They even had to halt production of the T-top cars (mine was) for a couple weeks so they could fix some issues with leaks. In fact, during this wait I had decided to transfer out to Utah with Ryder in July and the car still hadn't been built. The dealer worked with me and we were able to change the delivery point to Salt Lake City with another dealer doing the final setup. It was a long wait, but it was worth it. That was a great car and I kept it for 5 years and about 40000 miles! Had a lot of fun with it and it's a great classic car story!

Packing and Moving

We stopped only for food, gas and the restroom all the way back from Salt Lake. Our Wisconsin house had not been sold yet and we were considering what to do about it. We weren't back more than a couple days and got a call from a prospective buyer who just happened to be a Sheriff's Deputy for the county. He came over, checked around, and asked if he could bring his wife over. After she approved, he made an offer and we accepted. There was no way we could close on the house however, before I had to be out to Salt Lake City in two weeks. I ended up giving my wife power of attorney and she stayed in Wisconsin for an extra month to finish up. As the Camaro ran into production line problems and still hadn't been built, I was able to change the delivery to a Salt Lake City Chevy dealer.

So, two weeks later, we had a 29 foot U-haul truck filled up with all I could take, plus my motorcycle inside, towing a car behind and I was heading west to Utah! I started my new job on July 12, 1993 at Ryder Integrated Logistics' Swire Coca-Cola account in Salt Lake City, Utah!

I had just made the biggest change of my life by packing up and moving to Utah. Being pretty certain that the opportunity with Ryder and Coke was a good one, I wasn't too fearful. Our customer has sales centers throughout the intermountain west and the drivers, I found were pretty well satisfied and all went pretty smooth. I was able to settle in and enjoy my job traveling throughout the beautiful western states. We pulled Rocky Mountain Doubles (48' and 27' trailers) and Supersets (two 42' trailers), as well as 48 and 53 foot singles. Our main customer with production plants in Salt Lake City, Utah and Fruitland, Idaho is still one of the largest independent Coca Cola bottlers in the world.

Ryder has had this great customer since 1990 and as of 2020 they are one of the longest running continuous customers in Ryder history.

The early part of 1994, our Senior Logistics Manager's responsibilities were growing. Ryder had signed new business in Salt Lake, Las Vegas, Phoenix and other areas. They all were reporting to our Senior Manager in Salt Lake. At one of our safety meetings, he announced that he was looking for 4 drivers to step up and become Driver Trainers. The position would involve traveling to the other locations he was responsible for whenever needed for training, emergency relief driving, whatever was needed. While not driving, we were to help out in the recruitment, hiring and training of new drivers wherever and whenever they were needed. I submitted a resume to be considered and after an interview, I was picked as one of the four. So began my 24 years as a trainer!

The next nine years were quite a whirlwind in my life. Ryder's business was expanding rapidly and Craig's responsibilities were growing with accounts in Denver, Las Vegas, Phoenix and Seattle reporting to him. During some extended periods, we were traveling constantly, spending weeks at a time assisting at start-ups, hiring and training and backing up drivers at every location he was responsible for. We were so busy at one point, I did a start-up at a remote location by myself and flew to Medford, OR. I spent nearly a month meeting with the customer, hiring two drivers, equipping a couple of tractors, setting up the on board computers and training the drivers.

Sin City

Located about 400 miles south of Salt Lake City, I spent a lot of time working in Las Vegas in the 1990's. We had several customers down there that kept us busy, the Las Vegas Review Journal and Big O Tires were the largest. One summer we were down there so much my boss had an apartment rented for a few months so we could save on motel costs. Vegas is a fun place to visit but I could never live in that area. I found that many, if not most people permanently living and working there stay away from the casinos and avoid gambling. There are so many people that seem to have a constant chip on their shoulder and you have to watch your back around that town. People move to Vegas thinking they have found paradise but soon get caught up in drinking or gambling away most of their paychecks. Every casino had signs offering perks if you cashed your payroll check with them. One little known fact I found back then, there were almost as many U-haul trucks leaving the Las Vegas area every week as there were coming in.

At the Review Journal one sunny morning I was sitting in the streetside outdoor patio on MLK Boulevard with another trainer while some of the employees were taking a morning break. There was a fence between the street sidewalk and patio. About a dozen people were sitting at tables along with us when a couple gunshots rang out across the street. I thought it was someone setting off firecrackers at first, but all the employees immediately got up and went inside, and we followed. I was amazed that nobody really said much, like it was just a normal daily occurrence. They just walked over to the indoor cafeteria and continued their break. No-one even bothered to call the police!

Another afternoon, I was driving a rental car, returning to a motel after spending most of the day at a customer location. Approaching an intersection near downtown, the light turned red and I came to a stop and waited. I was in the left hand lane and a car pulled up on my right and stopped next to me. All of a sudden there were cars approaching from all directions screeching to a stop, unmarked patrol cars. Doors flew open and a bunch of police with assault rifles surrounded me and the other car. Thankfully their weapons were pointed at the other guy yelling at him not to move. Two cops pointed at me and motioned to get out of the way and drive on, which I was very glad to do. You never know what you'll come across in that town.

Seattle

Up in Seattle, in the mid-1990's, one of the major customers we signed was Eagle Hardware and Garden. At that time we had no other dedicated business in the Seattle area so my boss, along with me and two other trainers, flew up there for a month and began working out of our motel rooms. Starting with nothing, we had to locate office space to lease, buying everything from desks and chairs, computers, file cabinets, communication equipment and everything else necessary to get the operation going. My boss even had to hire and train a new logistics manager to oversee the operation and handle the drivers. Eagle also had remote store locations in Alaska and Hawaii, and later on, I spent five weeks on Oahu with Craig doing the start-up out there. Pretty intense stuff for a cheese-head truck driver from Wisconsin! While working with Craig in Hawaii, he received a promotion to Director of Customer Logistics! It was a special time and I was proud to be working for him. The one thing I will always be grateful to Craig for, is he taught me how to work and get things done. He was a hard man to keep up with but he was always willing to step in and do whatever he expected us to do. I found out that when you bust your butt and do a good job, you may be drop dead tired at the end of the day, but there is a lot of satisfaction in a job well done!

Oahu, Hawaii

As previously written, one of our major customers was Eagle Hardware and Garden, a Seattle based company. They had a chain of home improvement stores throughout the western states including Washington, Oregon, Utah and Colorado. Eagle also had two locations in Hawaii, one store on Oahu and the other on Maui.

The contract called for us to run the home delivery service for the stores out there also. After getting the mainland operations going I flew out with my boss, Craig, to get the startup going on Oahu. Neither of us knew anything about the place and it was up to me to find a motel for us to get started. Figuring the Holiday Inn right near the airport would be a central location and good for us, I made reservations. When I told the clerk how long we intended to be there, she upgraded my boss to a suite for the standard room rate. After making the long flight out and checking in over the weekend we discovered that the neighborhood was a pretty scary place, especially at night. That, along with airplane noise of taking off and landing, we weren't so happy,

The following Monday morning we had our first meeting with the local Eagle management people at their offices. After greetings and introductions someone asked us where we were staying. The look on their faces was priceless as they couldn't believe us two "haoles" chose the Airport Holiday Inn. It was pretty embarrassing for me as I had to admit that I picked the place. Someone stated " you'll get killed over there" and gave us the name of a nearby hotel that they had a corporate rate with. As soon as the meeting was over I called them and we moved that day. It was a beautiful hotel two blocks from the Waikiki beach and what a difference it indeed was!

I ended up staying five weeks on that first trip to get everything going. My wife was able to fly out for a week also at company expense. That can be good and bad because I had to still get a lot of work done while she was there and couldn't just take off and see the sites every day. I don't know that I would have ever gone to Hawaii for a vacation otherwise but it was an interesting place. Living there would never be an option for me but the weather was great. The cost of living is very high with many people having to work two jobs to get by. After the first few weeks I was starting to feel "closed in" with the small size of the island.

While my wife was out there the Ryder salesman that sold the account took a group of us Eagle and Ryder people out to a fancy rooftop restaurant for a celebratory meal that was memorable and during the time we were in Hawaii my boss, Craig, received a promotion to Director with Ryder. It was a lot of hard work but a heck of an experience.

Mountain Climbing in Bear Country with a Set of Doubles

One of our customers was Big O Tires out of Denver, Co. They had a central warehouse located in Henderson, Nevada. From there, we were delivering tires to their stores in Colorado, Arizona, northern and southern California. Because they were short handed with drivers on vacation, I went down for a week to help out.

The next afternoon I left out with a driver by the name of Chuck on a team run. He was an experienced driver but neither of us had been on that run before. We were to pull a set of triples on the interstate from Las Vegas to Grand Junction, Co. Upon arriving, we would drop the third trailer and continue with a set of doubles on state highways down through Delta, Montrose and Cortez delivering to the stores. The trailers were each 28 feet long. We had keys to a storage shed at each store where we could deliver their tires after hours. After helping make a store delivery late one night in Montrose, I went back in the sleeper while my co-driver started heading for Cortez. Needless to say, being in the heart of the Rocky Mountains and nowhere near an interstate highway, we were having to proceed carefully on the two lane state highways. Chuck drove south on State Hwy 145 which was the most direct route to Cortez. Neither of us had been on that highway before and it goes right past Telluride, a quite famous ski area in Colorado.

Being sound asleep in the berth, I woke up about 3am as the truck started bouncing around on some rough roads, going slower and slower. Pretty soon, I heard what sounded like gravel hitting the undercarriage and I knew we were not on a paved road. After sitting up, I opened the curtain and looked out the windshield to gaze at a very narrow gravel road that wasn't getting any wider. I hollered to Chuck, asking "where the hell are we?" His answer, "I think I made a wrong turn!" I then said, "well you better stop this thing because this road is getting narrower". He stopped the truck and I got out, the first thing I saw was a sign that said "Beware of Bears". We were on a dirt road going up a very heavily wooded mountainside. Jeez, at this point, I was pretty irate and not being very nice to poor Chuck. The road was so narrow that another vehicle wouldn't be able to get by us and we were pulling two trailers and not able to back up! He pulled the truck forward while I guided him to the absolute edge of the roadway with just enough clearance that I thought we could squeeze our tractor and lead trailer back past the other. We then disconnected the back trailer and proceeded up the mountain praying that we could find a place to get turned around. After about a quarter mile we found a spot where the edge was fairly firm and was able to jack the trailer back and forth enough to get it turned around. We then took that trailer back down, made it past the other and dropped it, while we went back to retrieve the other and hook them back up. I'm sure we spent at least 90 minutes trying to get ourselves out of that mess!

What happened was that Chuck didn't notice a sign as we approached Telluride telling him that he had to turn right to stay on State Hwy 145. He continued straight into and through the town on the only road that eventually ends at the top of a mountain! There is only one way out and that was to go back. As we were making our way back through town at about 4:30am we passed a town cop coming the other way who slammed on his brakes coming to a dead stop staring at us! I'm sure he was wondering what these two idiots were doing with a tractor and a set of doubles on a road that dead-ends at the top of a mountain. We were surprised that he didn't amuse himself by pulling us over. And no, Big O Tires does not have a store in Telluride, Colorado!

Team Driving

Sometime around 1996 or '97 my boss received word that seasonal extra help was needed for a national account customer. Their business involved transporting fresh cut floral greens and wreaths throughout the country to retail outlets. The Christmas season was their busy season and they were asking for volunteer drivers to spend six weeks running team to support their operation. They guaranteed $1,000 per week minimum to drivers that would commit.

I had just completed the orientation of a new young driver and was going to be riding with him for two weeks training anyway so I asked if he was interested and he said yes. He was trying to save up cash so he could move his wife and kid to Salt Lake City from Grealy, Co. He had left them there to come to Utah for a decent job and she was still employed at a meat packing plant in Colorado.

There were four of us drivers that agreed, making up two teams and off we went, getting a couple Ryder rental tractors and heading up to Belfair, Wa. We picked a couple of leased reefer trailers from a Ryder shop and pick up our loads. Leaving out Dave and I decided on running a 5 on, 5 off schedule. Being the first extended time for me running team, it was quite an experience. I hardly got any sleep the first couple days bouncing around in the sleeper. We had decent conventional Freightliners with air-ride but that made little difference. It was a real struggle until finally, I was so dead tired that my body had to sleep. Once past the initial couple days it was better, but still, team driving is a hard life. I don't know how they can do 10 on, 10 off with the new regulations.

After a couple weeks we were back up in the northwest getting loaded to go to Tennessee and I could sense that my partner was getting homesick missing his family. I had been thinking about running back through Salt Lake to get home for a couple hours but decided to go through Colorado so he could stop and see his wife. Well we drove up to their apartment and he introduced me to his wife. There was a definite tension between them so I went outside, telling Dave I would wait for him in the truck. A couple hours later Dave comes out and announces that he was quitting! The dude just walked off the truck on me, his wife telling him to either stay or leave for good. It's about midnight and I was pretty pissed off. He packed his stuff out and I just started driving, not wanting to wake my boss up, knowing she could do nothing at that time of night.

The next morning I called Michelle to tell her what happened. She called the account manager and they came up with a plan to fly another driver from Oklahoma into Kansas City where I could pick him up and he would finish out the commitment with me. Late that night I pulled into a truckstop near KC where he had taken a cab from the airport and picked him up. He got his stuff on board and I told him I would drive the first shift, 5 on, 5 off. One of the first things he said to me "I don't know how you can drive all night, I have problems staying awake". Not a good way to start off with me and I informed him what "team driving" consisted of. A short time later he says " I hope we don't go to New York, I'm wanted there". Needless to say, we didn't start out on very good terms.

We made it to the Nashville area where we delivered and then got stuck for three days while they looked for a load. That wasn't so bad though as we got a motel near the Nashville truck stop downtown and I was able to get away from my partner and tour the downtown honky tonks over the weekend. Being guaranteed $1,000 per week meant we didn't have to worry about getting the miles. By Monday, they still couldn't find us a load so we were told to dead-head to DeLand, Florida for another load of "greens". That load took us to Houston, the location of the customer's head-quarters. I had driven in and my partner was up for the next driv-ing shift. We spent several hours unloading and reloading for the northwest and I told him several times to jump in the sleeper and rest so he could be ready to go. I might as well have been talking to the wall as the jerk didn't listen to me.

Late in the afternoon they finished loading and I could tell he was tired. I was pretty irate and told him I would drive for a couple hours so he could sleep. After we switched out it was dark and I went back into the sleeper and dozed off. A couple hours later I was startled awake with the truck running on the gravel shoulder and violently veering off as dipshit jerked on the steering wheel. I tore open the curtain and asked him what the hell is going on with his response being "I got tired". That was it for me as my adrenaline took over telling him "pull over, I'm driving".

We were out in the middle of nowhere so I took the wheel until I could find a truckstop and payphone. I called my boss, told her what happened and said "either he gets off the truck or I will". That was it for Michelle also as she told me to take him to the Albuquerque airport and they would fly him back to where he came from. I never let him back behind the wheel and drove all night to get rid of him. When he woke up I told him what I had done and he remained quiet the rest of the way as I was in no mood for conversation. After getting rid of him I called Michelle and found that the other team from Salt Lake wanted to split up and that Jim was willing to jump on my truck to finish out the six weeks. What a relief! Jim was another driver trainer from our account and a true professional. We got along great and finished out the time together. Ever since then, I've had no desire to ever run team again! A note about young Dave: About a year later, he showed up at our office wanting to know if he could reapply for a job. "Ummm, no!" was the response.

Terror Ride with Art!

As previously written, before Lowes bought them out, one of our customers was Eagle Hardware and Garden, a chain of home improvement stores based in Seattle. We had a contract to do the curbside home delivery of building materials and inside appliance setup to their customers. The delivery trucks that we used were day cab tandem axle tractors pulling 32 foot curtain-sided flatbed trailers. Attached to the back of the trailers were forklift trucks that were needed to offload lumber and building materials to the curb. As you can imagine, with the 8,000 pound weight of a forklift hanging off the back, these trucks handled very poorly in wet or slippery conditions! Especially if you didn't have a load on the trailer. Because we also delivered and set up appliances for Eagle's customers in their homes, we had a helper along with a driver on each truck.

One winter day, one of the helpers was sick so I had to ride along with Art, who was a regular driver for us servicing customers of the four Eagle stores in the Salt Lake City area. We went to a store in the morning, loaded up and proceeded to make the local deliveries scheduled for that day. There was a snow storm forecast to be moving in that afternoon, so we wasted no time in trying to get our deliveries completed. Our last stop of the day was a few miles north of Salt Lake in a fancy neighborhood located on the "benches" of the Wasatch mountain range. There were some pretty steep hills in the area and it took awhile to find the address. As we were inside the house doing an appliance setup for the customer, it began snowing. After finishing up, we went outside to find the streets and sidewalks covered with an inch or so of the white stuff. We got in the truck and with Art driving, we started to make our way out of the neighborhood and back to the freeway. We turned a corner and were suddenly headed down a very steep hill on a residential street that was not very wide, lined with trees and mailboxes and a couple of parked cars.

Although we were only doing a couple of miles an hour, we both seemed to sense it at the same time. The weight of the forklift on the back was actually starting to push the trailer sideways! We both looked out the mirrors at the same time and Art proceeded to take action while I started looking for something to hang on to! Of course the first thing he tried was the brakes and countersteering, but immediately, he knew that was just going to jack knife us. So he came off the brake and floored the throttle. I was looking out the mirror and the truck was starting to straighten out but now our speed was picking up and it was a long way to the bottom of the hill. As soon as the trailer started to straighten out Art jammed on the brakes trying to scrub off speed until the trailer started coming sideways again, only this time to my side. Floor throttle again, straighten out and hit the brakes! I was hanging on wondering which tree or mailbox and how many we were going to take out when I looked a little further down the hill and "Holy Crap"! There's a minivan full of kids with a woman driving it, coming towards us! I looked out the mirror again and saw the trailer coming to Art's side again, thinking "Oh God, we're going to take out the minivan"!

Everything seemed to be going in slow motion. I remember having the thought "How are we going to explain this to the boss?"

Art mashed the throttle again and the trailer straightened out just enough to get by that poor woman. She was stopped and I'll never forget the look of terror on her face with her mouth wide open as we went by. Finally, the hill started to level out and Art was able to make a left turn as we were sliding through an intersection! During the whole ordeal, we never said a word to each other, knowing that he was a professional (and I certainly wasn't going to distract him!).

After he got the rig under control, I practically punched him on the arm and asked him where the "hell" he learned to drive like that? His response was that he was an old log hauler and had to handle trucks coming out of the woods on slippery and hilly trails. I've always considered myself to be a skillful driver but that was one fancy piece of driving he did that afternoon.

I think that there are very few drivers that could have come out of that without an accident! I don't know if I could have. Tip of the hat to Art M.!

For several years we did all the home deliveries for the Eagle stores throughout the western U.S., Hawaii and Alaska. They were happy with our service but unfortunately the owner decided to sell out his company to Lowes. Since Lowes' corporate thinking was to do their own customer deliveries without third party logistics, our contract was not renewed. I ended up making three trips to Hawaii, one for startup, one for driver and management meetings and training, and the last to shut it down. It was a disappointing end, but it was a great adventure.

Throwing Tires in Phoenix

One of the not so pleasant responsibilities I had as a driver trainer back in the mid-1990's was having to be ready to travel and being on-call basically 24/7. We were trained for emergency backup at every location that my company director level boss oversaw throughout the intermountain west. About 90 miles west of Salt Lake City across the border of Nevada is the casino town of Wendover. Occasionally my wife and I would go out there for the weekend and stay over in a motel, driving back on Sunday. This was in the days before everyone had cell phones and I had to wear a company provided pager.

One Sunday morning back in the mid-1990's we were driving back from Wendover and my pager started beeping about 70 miles west of Salt Lake. Because of the remote area in the west desert I had been out of range most of the way home. I stepped it up, got home and called my "Director" boss to find out what was going on. He told me that a shuttle driver for our Big O Tire account out of Phoenix had been in a serious accident coming back from Las Vegas. They had no one to cover the local deliveries to the Phoenix area stores the next morning, which was Monday. I had to get on the phone and reserve a ticket for the next flight to Phoenix out of Salt Lake and get a motel room. Within an hour I was headed to the airport to jump on a plane.

After arriving and getting a rental car, I went to the shop, got the keys, paperwork and looked over the truck and trailer I had to drive in the morning. At the motel I spent the evening going over the delivery route, studying maps and writing directions to get to the stores I needed to deliver. For my added anticipation, it was summertime in Phoenix.

I got up about 4:30am, went outside to find it had cooled down overnight to about 90 degrees. The driver's job once arriving at the tire store was to get the tires to the back of the trailer with store personnel stacking and putting them in inventory. Even so, throwing tires off a trailer in 108 degree heat can be dangerous if you're not acclimated to the weather and out of condition for that type of work. With the sun beating on the van trailer and no air circulation the temperature had to be extreme. Thankfully, I knew the importance of staying hydrated and was stocked up with large bottles of water that I was constantly drinking from. Still at the end of that first day, I was completely exhausted. I got back to the room and took a long cool shower, ordered room service, and tried to recuperate to do it all over again the next day.

That was one miserable week I had before they were able to get another driver to cover the run. Thankfully, a little front came through on the second day and high temperatures stayed in the low 100's. But, at the end of the week, I was more than happy to be back on a plane at Sky Harbor Airport and heading back to Salt Lake City.

The life of a driver trainer was not always pleasant. My car trunk always contained a pillow, sleeping bag and a change of clothes along with driving and raingear to be ready to jump in a truck at a moment's notice. With a company provided credit card, I was prepared for instant air travel, rental cars and motels.

My Ride-along with Saddam Hussein's Soldier

The year 1999 was a crazy one, I spent almost all of the summer working in Phoenix. Ryder had signed new business with three customers and I had to be down there on startups helping get dozens of drivers hired, oriented and trained. One of the accounts was for a customer that involved night deliveries to convenience stores using straight trucks. The minimum experience required of the drivers we hired was not as stringent as it was for tractor trailer drivers, needing only a minimum of one year in a "like" vehicle, a Class B CDL license and good driving record.

I remember reviewing this driver's application, interviewing and road testing him, nothing unusual got my attention. I knew he was of Middle Eastern descent but really didn't pay much attention. After the orientation process, I rode along with him on the route for a few days to get him trained up. He had a pretty thick accent and I really had to listen carefully to be able to understand him. One night as we were driving along I asked him what country he was from originally and he said "Iraq". Well, this was well before 9/11 and from what I knew about Iraq, it was the country ruled by Saddam Hussein that invaded Kuwait back in the early 90's during the first President Bush's term in office. During a short war, we kicked their butts all the way back to Baghdad and they supposedly surrendered. I can't remember this driver's name, but he then told me that he had been in the Iraq war. I said "you fought against Saddam?" and he said "no, I was in Saddam's Army".

That statement was quite a shock to me and I had all these thoughts racing through my head about how the hell could he have ended up here in the United States. and wondering if I'm riding along in a truck with some crazy terrorist driving it! I'm not kidding when I say that was a very unsettling feeling for a bit.

After thinking for a few moments, I finally asked "you mean you fought against us?" In fractured English, he replied "oh yes, but I surrendered". I said "you surrendered to the United States?" and he said "yes". I then replied with "well, how the hell did you end up here?" He then followed up with a fascinating story of how every young male in Iraq was forced into military service and the only reason for a lot of them to be in was to avoid torture or imprisonment. He told me he was no Saddam supporter and scared to death of the US military. The first chance he had, he went running up to a US patrol waving a white towel and surrendered. I asked what happened after that and he said they interrogated him and put him in prison for three years. After about three years, the officials determined that he was not a threat to us and asked him what he wanted to do. He could not go back to Iraq as he would certainly be killed for deserting. His mother and the rest of his family had no contact with him all the years after his surrender and thought he had been killed in the war. He was offered the opportunity to come to the United States and he took it.

After arriving here, he went to Phoenix, found a job and started working his way up and making a life for himself. I remember him saying that he had wished so much for us to go all the way into Baghdad and finish off Saddam when we had the chance. He was longing for the day he could see his mom and family again. As long as Saddam was still in power, he could not go home and I hope he was able to accomplish that. He was a decent guy. Some of the people you meet by chance in life can be amazing!

What Drives Driver Trainers Crazy

Being a driver trainer with my company, Ryder, for 24 years was different from what most other company's trainers do. I've always considered myself to be very fortunate, not actually having to teach new tractor trailer drivers to drive, as our company hires only experienced "professionals". Of course there are a wide variety of truck drivers and they all have varying levels of experience, but the people we hired during my time had a safe work and driving history and knew how to drive. We rode along to train drivers in our system, as in operating the on-board computer, paperwork, yard and delivery procedures, etc.

Back in the early 1980's, I went through the Diesel Driving School in Sun Prairie, Wisconsin to get my training. We had an old, grumpy trainer that would ride along in the passenger seat nicknamed Red. Every time I did something wrong behind the wheel, he would punch me on the arm, scaring the crap out of me. But it sure taught me not to make the same mistake again! In my class of 29 students, I graduated ranked number one. In this day and age, probably not a good idea to be punching your students! After having been a trainer for so many years I wrote down a list of things that got me cranky while riding with new drivers:

If you are bob-tailing a tractor, why would anyone start in first or second and shift through every gear in the transmission? How long has it been taught that with electronic engines, you should start out in the highest gear that will get the truck rolling without using the throttle. Starting in first or second while bob-tailing or empty is ridiculous, wastes fuel and bounces me back and forth in the passenger seat. Although I can understand a trainee not wanting to skip gears while driving with a trainer. They have a lot to think about and don't want to get "lost" in the transmission.

I realize that every truck is different and it takes some time to shift it smoothly. Drivers are not used to having a trainer ride with them and are understandably nervous. If you can't pick it up right away, try using the clutch! Seems like everyone insists on "floating" the gears, missing shifts and constantly grinding gears, making me cranky. You can shift a lot smoother, until you get more comfortable, by using that left leg.

Loading docks and yards are often congested and can overwhelm drivers that are not used to it. As we enter a yard that my driver is not familiar with, I try to give information on where to drop trailers or which door to back in. All the years of backing experience have taught me that properly positioning your rig before backing is half the battle. If you can position your rig to back straight into a dock instead of jackknifing, it makes for a lot less work and a much safer move. It amazes me at some who do not take a moment to think about where they are going, and how to line up for a backing maneuver.

Drive it like you normally drive! I have been a professional driver for over thirty years and expect a driver I'm riding with to drive like a normal professional. Crawling around like a grandma and driving 5 or 10 miles per hour below the speed limit to demonstrate that you are a safe driver does not work for me. I know how you will drive after I leave the truck and have witnessed it hundreds of times. We hire drivers with a safe working history and we know you are a safe driver.

We provide map books for every new driver that show routes and directions for every place we normally go. When training a driver, we know the day before where we will be going the following day. Now, I would think that if it were me, going somewhere I haven't been before, I would at least look at the maps the night before to plan a route. I've had a couple drivers hook their trailers up in the yard, ready to leave and ask me if which direction (north or south) out of Salt Lake! That makes me crazy.

Training new drivers on local routes almost always means an early morning start time. I tell each driver what time we need to meet to pick up the tractor. Now, if I was a new employee, I would make damn sure to not be late during my training period. When I get up at 3:30am, drive to work and sit twiddling my thumbs, waiting for my trainee to show up, it does not start my day well. In fact, I got so mad one time that I told the guy if he was late getting up again with me, to not bother showing up at all. And he didn't, with another trainer he was scheduled to go with. That trainer called him at home and gave him another chance. I would have left his ass sit home and did the run without him. He only lasted a few weeks after that.

My Dream Car

Fortunately, after the first couple years, I have always been able to make decent money in trucking. That allowed me to be able to enjoy driving some great cars throughout my life. Previously, I

wrote about the 1993 Z-28 Camaro that I owned and what a great car it was. It had the LT-1 Corvette engine with 275 horsepower and had impressive performance.

About 1996 and '97, I started reading about the upcoming redesign of the Corvette for the 1998 model year. From the ground up, the C5 was to be all new and would be powered by the next generation LS-1 engine putting out 345 horsepower! Well that got me thinking about Corvettes again, but I had a wife and it would take a lot of work to convince her that we "needed a new Corvette"! It took a year and I waited for the '98s to come out to read the reviews. After selling the Camaro in late 1997, I drove an old beater 1984 Camaro for a while to save up some cash and started doing the research.

After the experience I had trying to buy that '93 Camaro at a decent price, I figured the dealer sharks would be out to make a killing again. Boy, was I correct! I visited every Chevy dealer in the Salt Lake City area and was given the same song and dance. They were selling every single Corvette they could get their hands on and for several thousand dollars over the "sticker" price! There was no way I was going to get ripped off like that and decided to wait it out. I was even calling dealers all over the country to see if they would deal.

I then called Joe Banaszak, the Chevy dealer back in Crivitz, Wisconsin who gave me such a good deal on the '93 Camaro. After talking to him and offering to pay $2000 over his invoice cost on a Corvette, he quickly agreed. A few hours later, he called back with bad news. Chevrolet told him that all dealers were only allowed to order Corvettes based on their previous sales. Since this dealer had not sold any the previous year, he would not even be able to order one! You can imagine, I was pretty incensed after receiving this information. I thanked him for his efforts, told him I was not going to be ripped off and would wait as long as was necessary. I asked him to call me if the market changed and he would be permitted to order. This all took place during the spring and summer of 1998 and I pretty much resigned myself to the idea that it would be quite a while before I would be able to purchase one.

Along came the beginning of winter, December of 1998. They had started producing the 1999 model year cars in September. Still searching newspaper ads nearly every day, I came across a simple ad in the Salt Lake Tribune. Basically a one or two line ad that said "1999 Corvette on sale, $38,995.00" and a phone number. I thought, surely this had to be a used car that someone decided they couldn't afford. I called the number and it was a Chevy dealer about 30 miles away in Toelle. After asking whether this was a used vehicle, a salesman replied " No, it's brand new and sitting on the showroom floor!" I then asked him if the price quoted was correct, he said yes and I told him I was on my way. After asking permission to leave work, I ran home, got my wife and raced out there.

The car had everything I would have ordered on it, the sticker price in the window was about $44,500.00! Keep in mind that I searched all over the country and everyone was paying a couple thousand over sticker for them. We weren't there five minutes before I agreed to the purchase. A couple hours later, after getting it out of the showroom, I drove that thing home! And I was a really happy guy, closing out the '90s driving my dream car.

A while later I found out why the dealership had made such a good deal on that Corvette. They were in financial trouble, it was the beginning of winter (not a good selling season for Corvettes) and they were paying interest for that expensive car in their showroom. It wasn't long after, they went out of business. I think I got the deal of a lifetime on that car and sure had a lot of fun with it. Chevrolet did a great job on the C5 model, I kept it almost 5 years and it's a great classic car story. Unfortunately, I had to sell it in 2003 after getting divorced. Wish I still had that car!

A Note About Frigo Cheese

A couple years after I left Wisconsin in 1993, Frigo Cheese in Lena suffered a devastating fire that nearly destroyed the entire complex. They were owned by Stella Foods of Illinois at the time and employed about 400 people. The entire population of Lena was less than 600 people! That was in January of 1996. Thankfully, with a $750,000.00 grant from the state of Wisconsin, they rebuilt the facility and were able to reopen within about six months. In 1997 Saputo Cheese USA acquired Stella Foods and the Frigo brand name. As of 2020 they are still operating the plant in Lena, Wisconsin.

THE 2000'S

Throughout the rest of the 1990's and into the early 2000's, I was traveling a tremendous amount of time. In the early 2000's, Ryder reorganized, moved teams around and Craig left for a role as Vice-President at another company. Having spent all those years traveling, I was more than ready to spend more time at home! Our customer has production centers in Salt Lake City and Idaho and we kept plenty busy with about 50 drivers handling their transportation needs. In 2012 we added a couple of drivers that were domiciled in Phoenix. In fact, I spent a couple weeks down there training and that was the first time in years that I had to fly anywhere. So, life goes on and all in all, I can say that so far, I've had a pretty good trucking career! In fact, it must have been good, as I married a truck driver!

Through most of the 1990's and into early 2000's my job involved extensive travel as a Driver Trainer for Ryder. Being gone so much was starting to take a toll on me and fortunately things started to slow down a bit. Our local Director of Logistics, Craig, left the company in 2003 for an opportunity as Vice President at another logistics company. Ryder then reorganized somewhat, moving some of his former assigned geographic areas to different teams. Most of my travel stopped and I was able to focus more on our core team of drivers in Salt Lake City and Idaho. My primary boss, Michelle, was now a Senior Logistics Manager.

About March of 2002, we were looking to put a couple of drivers on to be ready for the busy summer season. We had an ad in the newspaper and were taking applications. One of the drivers we brought on board was a woman named Mary. We went through the orientation and I rode with her quite a bit the first couple weeks for training. She was a good driver, did a great job and got along with everyone. In the five months she was with us, I never heard anyone (drivers, customers or managers) say a bad word about her. She was well liked and, when she announced that she had to resign after 5 months, it was a shock to everyone. She was married at the time and her husband was not happy with the erratic work schedule she had. Everyone was sorry to see her leave, including myself.

About five years later, in September of 2007, I was sitting at my desk doing paperwork and I looked up to see Mary standing in the doorway. I was quite surprised and after a short conversation, learned that she came in looking for a job. We had an opening for another driver, so she filled out an application and I got to work on it as soon as she left. Our senior manager happened to be on vacation but I knew she would not hesitate to bring Mary back, if we could qualify her. The other two managers were in favor also. She had made a reference to being divorced somewhere on her application and that sure started me thinking. I had gotten divorced in 2003 with the idea that I would never, ever be interested in getting married again. Having been alone for five years, I was living in a nice fifth wheel trailer and was pretty comfortable.

So, it took a couple weeks to get her background info and all the paperwork done. I rode with her the first week to refresh her on the procedures and paperwork. This time, I was trying to find out a lot more about her. This was pretty sneaky, but I remember asking one of our supervisors to make sure I was the only one to train her the first week! The more I found out, the more I liked her and by the end of the week, I figured what the heck, I'm going to ask her out. The worst that could happen was for her to say no. And she did! On a Friday afternoon, she said no. That upcoming weekend was surely a miserable one that I spent alone. She was scheduled to be turned loose to go by herself the following Monday, but at the last minute, they scheduled me to ride with her for two more days.

So, on Monday morning we met up and I apologized for putting her in a bad situation. My intent had been to ask her out after her training was done, so as not to put any pressure on her, but they scheduled us two extra days. I think I ended up riding with her for most of the week and I left the issue alone and didn't mention it again. At the end of our last day together, she said she would go out with me. We got married about a year later back in Wisconsin in September, 2008.

Unfortunately, our marriage ended in 2016. The split was amicable and I will always miss some of the great times we had along with all of my Utah step-family who welcomed me into their lives. I am now retired, moved back to my home state of Wisconsin, in a great relationship and enjoying the last chapter of my life. All in all, I've been a very fortunate man.

Leaving Utah

In February, 2018 I wrote in my blog: *"In a couple days, after retiring the first of this year, I am moving back to my home state of Wisconsin. I've spent almost 25 years living and working in Utah and it's been* *quite a ride. This move is with mixed feelings, knowing I will always miss this place."*

Update May, 2020: After my marriage ended in 2016, I was almost 64 years old and my priorities had to undergo significant change. I really had no family out west and needed to start preparing for retirement. My mom was still alive in a memory care facility in Wisconsin and the cost of living in Utah was astronomical compared to rural northern Wisconsin. So I made the decision to move back after I pulled the plug. Part of this was written as a good-bye post to Utah in my blog in early 2018.

Thanks to my dear friends back in Wisconsin I found a nice 3.3 acre wooded property with a large garage and A-frame house near Crivitz and closed on it November of 2017. Then all I had to do was find a buyer of my double-wide mobile home in a 55 and over restricted park in Salt Lake. That took a while as the park had been bought out and they were drastically raising the lot rents to unbelievable rates. After finally finding a buyer and closing at the end of February, 2018 I was ready to go back to Wisconsin, the same way I left 25 years ago.

"After having been a regional semi-driver from Wisconsin since 1980, I transferred to Salt Lake City with Ryder in July of 1993 driving a 24 foot U-haul truck with all my possessions, pulling a car and tow dolly behind. Coming across I-80 in Iowa I had to detour many miles off the interstate due to flooded roads from the huge winter storms of early 1993. Back on I-80, in the western side of Nebraska, just east of Wyoming, I ran into a thunderstorm and saw an empty semi-truck with a husband-wife team get blown sideways in a microburst and flip over only a few hundred feet in front of me. Thankfully, both were unhurt

and able to climb out the top through the passenger door of the cab-over as I pulled up. They were pretty shook up and I had never seen anything like that before. Coming down Parley's canyon into the Salt Lake valley with that U-haul and tow vehicle behind was a whole different experience than with my car a few weeks earlier! I remember having thoughts, wondering what I was getting myself into.

Being from the midwest, I didn't know what a mountain was until Boyce, Bob and other drivers coached me through a few canyons, my wide eyes staring and white knuckles on the wheel! Utah is a special place to live and work, having traveled and spent extensive time as a trainer in cities throughout the intermountain west. There is nowhere I'd rather live other than in a cabin in the north woods of Wisconsin, getting back to a small town quiet life, near family and friends."

Both Boyce Williams (79) and Bob Carter (80) passed away in 2019. Bob was a fellow driver trainer with me for many years from 1994 until he retired. Boyce had been selected as Ryder Systems corporate Driver of the Year and had well over 2 million miles accident free.

"There are so many people I'd like to acknowledge, I'll miss them, fellow drivers, supervisors, employees and vendors of our customer. I've worked with so many people in Las Vegas, Phoenix, Seattle, Denver and elsewhere. A lot of great friends, the list would be long and thanks to Facebook, I can hopefully stay in touch. Most of all, thanks to my "Utah family" of the last 10 years, who always made me feel welcome and I will forever love and miss! Thanks for all of the great memories. The circle of life pulls me back to Wisconsin, but my time here has been so special! Oh, and by the way, I will never miss being stuck in Wyoming weather...... and that's all I got to say about that, LOL. I hope the drive

back (in another U-Haul and my car on a tow dolly) will have a lot less drama than the first one coming here. Take care!"

The End

It's been almost two and a half years now since I retired. I'm in a great relationship and content. Now, in the middle of this Covid-19 mess, I'm sure glad I don't have to work. I really don't miss driving for work but did find a good deal on a used 36-foot motorhome last year with a car to tow behind. I guess you can't keep a natural driver in one place for too long. We were able to escape the Wisconsin winter and spend three months in Florida this year. We had a great time and hope to repeat annually.

All in all, trucking has given me the opportunity to have a good life. It was a lot of hard work but I always made decent money and have enough put away for a comfortable retirement. I don't know what the future holds for professional drivers and trucking, but, if you keep your record clean, there are good companies to work for. Unlike some, I have never had the desire to own my own truck and be self-employed. I've seen so many do this and slowly go broke. Company drivers get a lot in the way of benefits and vacation that owner operators do not. But for some, it can work out. If you choose to be a professional driver, good luck with your endeavor, drive safe and get onboard with a good company. You can make some very good money if you are a true "professional".

One thing for newer drivers to remember: It may take some time to get on with a good trucking company. Those that take on higher risk drivers do not usually pay well, may have poor equipment or sporadic work. Whatever you do, do not quit without notice. It's not worth screwing up your work history because you're angry and want to walk off a job. I've reviewed thousands of driver applications and saw it all the time, nearly doing it myself once. It will make any prospective employer think twice about you and possibly pass you over for someone else.

Usually the best companies are hard to get into, so you have to work at it. The market for drivers is always cyclical but an old trucker friend once told me "Drivers are a dime a dozen but good ones are always hard to find". My employer for more than 25 years was Ryder Integrated Logistics, they have locations all over the country. Happy Trucking! Keep reading for a bonus section:

CLASSIC CAR
Short Stories

1970 Pontiac GTO - Dick
hands me the keys!

While in high school, I had a job pumping gas at a Clark filling station. I wasn't yet 18 years old when I graduated in the spring of 1970 and started working third shift full time afterwards.

A guy by the name of Dick worked third shift part-time on weekends. He was in his 30's, married and had a full time job as a semi-truck driver during the week. Due to my working third shift Sunday through Thursday nights, I kept pretty much the same sleep schedule on weekends. Spending considerable time hanging out at the station when he was working, we became good friends. He was a great guy with a good sense of humor and became almost like a father figure to me, giving me a lot of good advice about life and how to handle myself growing up.

Dick worked hard and played hard. The reason he had the part-time job was for extra money that he could buy his toys with. One Friday night he came for the start of his 10pm shift driving a brand new 1970 dark green Pontiac GTO! It had the 400 cubic inch V8 and four speed transmission and was a great looking car. With hood scoops and rally wheels, I think it also had a Hurst shifter in it. Back in those days, we didn't know many people who could buy a brand new car and this was quite a shock, Dick became the center of attention for a while with his new muscle car.

A few weeks later I was at the station one Saturday night hanging out. It got to be about 1am in the morning and said to Dick that I was going to go out and pick up a sandwich at a Suburpia sub shop before they closed. I asked him if he wanted anything and he said "sure". He reached in his pocket to take out some money, handing it to me along with his car keys! "Go ahead and take my car", he said as I stood there dumbfounded. I couldn't believe he would let me drive his pride and joy (especially without him in it) and thought he was joking at first. I stammered something trying to say thanks and told him I would drive it safely.

So I nervously went out and got into his car. I started the motor and concentrated really hard to let the clutch out easy so I wouldn't look like a fool and stall the engine. That trip to the sub shop was surely a memorable one. I remember the car feeling so powerful on the freeway. Barely moving the throttle the car would effortlessly accelerate. I downshifted into third gear and mashed the gas pedal, shifted back to 4th, and it rocketed to over 90 MPH seemingly in an instant. Not knowing at the time, it was the first year the GTO had "variable ratio" power steering and a rear anti-roll bar and I remember noticing how well it steered and handled. It was quite unlike the 1968 Plymouth GTX that I had an opportunity to drive and did a story on.

Being so grateful he let me drive his car that I didn't dare abuse it by burning rubber or driving carelessly but I did get on the throttle a few times and was able to feel the power. The new car smell, sound and power, I'm sure, were contributing factors convincing me to spend a hell of a lot of money on cars for most of my life! What a cool experience and one I will never forget. In fact, that was the first time I had ever driven a "new" car (barely broken in) and it was a 1970 Pontiac GTO! How cool is that for a gas pump jockey just barely out of high school making about $2.00 per hour? And more than a decade later, I chose professional truck driving as a second career, and did it for more than 37 years.

What happened to Dick? A while later, the company he drove semi-truck for went bankrupt and he lost his full time job. He was tired of driving anyway and ended up getting a job waiting tables at an upscale restaurant. We all felt sorry for him. But, as I said, Dick worked hard and played hard. Within an amazingly short period of time he ended up managing the place!

Driving My Buddy's '68 Plymouth 440 GTX

AKA, the "gentleman's" muscle car!

Back while we were still in high school, my friend Ross's brother bought a brand new 1968 Plymouth GTX. He was several years older than us, had a decent job and could afford to buy a new car. It was a great looking dark "Race Green" color with the hood scoops and racing stripe along the side. It had the 375 HP 440 cubic inch motor in it with a Torqueflite automatic transmission. Both Ross and I had 1962 Chevy Impalas and we sure were envious of his awesome car.

The Plymouth GTX was introduced as the Belvedere GTX in 1967 by the Plymouth division to be a "gentleman's" muscle car. The Road Runner was a cheaper, bare bones twin which came standard with the 383 cu.in. motor and outsold the GTX more than two to one. Using the Belvedere trim, it had less insulation and fewer comfort items (padding, vinyl roof, trim), which reduced weight, helped produce better track times, and kept it in the low price field.

Several years later, in the early 1970's, Ross ended up buying that car from his brother. It was still in decent shape and I remember riding around as a passenger in it, listening to the great sound of that big block 440 engine. Ross took great care of his vehicles and didn't care to abuse them and I don't remember him burning rubber or going all out in it while I was with him.

One night he offered to let me use the car and keep it overnight. The reason I needed it is another story in itself, but I gladly accepted the chance to drive it! As I took off down the street and made the first turn at a corner, I was astonished at the effort it took to turn the steering wheel! The car had no power steering, which I knew about, but the weight of that big cast iron 440 and automatic on the front end sure made it an arm workout to go around a corner. He had one of those leather wraps around the edge of the steering wheel to enable a better grip on it.

Those big Mopars were built to go fast in a straight line down a quarter mile track, not for a race course. But go in a straight line it could and it was thrilling when I got a chance to "open it up" a couple of times. I didn't go burning rubber with it, as I knew how Ross took care of his cars. The acceleration and sound of that GTX was awesome. But I tell you what, I would have had second thoughts about throwing that car into a corner sideways and being able to come out of it in one piece with that steering.

But I sure would love to get the chance to drive another one. What a blast!

Uncle Jim's Volkswagen Beetle

1960's Beetle / Snow Machine Extraordinaire

In a previous story I wrote about my uncle taking me on my first road trip and the effect he had on some of the decisions I've made in my life. That got me thinking about another time after getting my driver's license when he let me drive his mid-1960's Volkswagen beetle.

Uncle Jim joined the US Marines and after he got out of the service about 1960 or '61 bought himself a Corvette convertible, driving that for a while before meeting a girl, getting married and having a kid. With a baby on the way, he had to sell the car and ended up buying a Hudson. What a letdown for me when he drove up to our house in that thing! He didn't spend money foolishly after that and was always looking for ways to save a buck. They bought a house about 30 miles west of Milwaukee in Nashotah, Wisconsin to settle down and raise their family. I remember dad driving us out for family visits and it seemed to take forever to get there. Jim had to commute to Milwaukee to work every day and started looking for ways to cut his expenses.

One day, he came driving up to our house in a Volkswagen Beetle that he bought in the 1960's. I don't remember if it was new or used but he raved to my dad about how inexpensive it was and how much gas he saved by driving it. We had a couple of '57 Chryslers with 392 cubic inch Hemi engines that got about 10 miles per gallon. He ended up buying another Beetle and had two of them at one point. Unfortunately, he had some major problems with at least one of the cars and had to have a motor rebuild or replacement.

I must have been about 17 years old, the car was in a repair shop in Milwaukee and scheduled to be ready for pickup on a Friday that Uncle Jim and his wife were going to be out of town. It was winter, December I think, and he asked me if I would pick up the car for him and keep it over the weekend and I said "sure". He needed to have the car for work on Monday morning and the shop would be closed when they got home Sunday. He told me I could go ahead and use the car if I wanted, and I did!

After getting my driver's license at 16, I kind of inherited the family car, a 1957 Chrysler New Yorker that had a Hemi engine. This was after my dad bought another '57 Chrysler (Imperial) with the same engine. Up to that point all the cars that I had ever driven were front engine, rear wheel drive. I was used to handling these cars in snow. As my brother wrote in one of my previous posts: "The reason is that it was mom who took Dan and me to the Arlen's shopping center parking lot at night so many times to practice driving, including sliding around on snow, at age 14 and 15. Front wheel drive cars were very rare at that time.

That Beetle was the first car I had ever driven with the engine in the back of the car. Well it just so happened that on the following day, Saturday, it began to snow and it kept snowing through the afternoon and evening, piling up quite a few inches on the streets. I drove the car someplace that evening and couldn't believe how well it handled in the snow. With the weight of the engine over the back wheels, and the overall light weight of the vehicle, traction was unbelievable and I felt I could drive through anything. I had a blast driving that thing all over town, it must have been several hours! I actually had to stop and put more gas in the car. It had a manual 4 speed tranny and to me, seemed as much fun as driving a go-cart around on a slippery track. The one bad thing I remember is that the windshield defroster was practically useless in that kind of weather. Those cars were notorious for having a crappy heater/defroster system. I had to take a big rag with me, constantly having to wipe the inside of the windshield so I could see. I actually went back home to get that rag so I could go out for more fun! I also remember the wipers not working very well in the snow, having to stop frequently to clean the ice buildup off of them.

I'm not sure that Uncle Jim would have approved of my antics that night, but I had so much fun with that little car! I wasn't abusing it and didn't crash it, so that was the important thing.

Thanks for the ride Uncle Jim!

My Hemi Chrysler

All during my teenage years, I was a big fan of Chrysler products. About 1962, my dad bought a used 1957 Chrysler New Yorker with a 392 cubic inch hemi motor in it, so I naturally was really into the Mopar stuff! My best friend's dad owned a Ford, so naturally he was a Ford guy and I was all Mopar.

The New Yorker was the family car for several years and I kind of "inherited" it when I got my driver's license at 16 and my dad bought another 1957 Chrysler, this one a more luxurious Imperial with leather seats, power windows and the same 392 hemi motor in it. For 1957 the 392 cubic inch hemi came standard with a Carter 4-barrel carburetor and was rated at 325 horsepower. There was an optional dual 4-barrel setup offered on the Chrysler 300 that upped the horsepower to 375. The 1957 models also came with the TorqueFlite 3-speed push button automatic transmission and a torsion bar suspension called Torsion-Aire that gave smoother handling and ride quality to the car. The '57 was also offered as a convertible and they are extremely rare (only about 1,000 produced).

Unfortunately, the New Yorker was pink with a white top! I remember my reaction the first time I saw the car. My mom and us kids were at my Aunt and Uncle's house visiting when my dad called and said he had bought a car. He announced that he was going to drive it over to pick us up and I was eagerly watching out the front window to see when he pulled up. Eventually he drove up in this huge 4-door sedan that was PINK with a white top. I was horrified! But my dad was so proud of his purchase. The car was actually so long that it would not fit in our garage on 19th and Chambers in Milwaukee! Dad had to extend the door hinges out a few inches in order to squeeze it in. He bought it from a retired couple and it was a very low mileage car. I think my dad's taste in car colors was questionable at the time. The Imperial he bought was kind of a weird burnt orange color with a white top!

Eventually, getting older, more interested in cars and used to the color, I was very impressed when I found out what was under the hood. That big car had a huge amount of torque and horsepower compared to most of the cars of it's day, and could bury that 120 MPH speedometer needle with no problem! If you gave it much more than half throttle starting out from a stop it would squeal the tires. The car had dual exhausts and I installed some chrome tips as well as "Hemi Powered" stickers to put on the sides. My father was pretty amused and just shook his head! You wouldn't believe how many times I had to open the hood to prove to someone that there really was a hemi under there!

Dad lost his sense of humor though, after I discovered how to do "power-stands". That is when you brake with your left foot while flooring the throttle, thereby doing a very smokey burnout of the rear wheels. I was doing this in front of our high school one day, showing off, and broke a u-joint! My dad came and we towed it to our neighbor's house, who was a mechanic. I had told my dad that the u-joint had just "come apart". Well, after the mechanic inspected it, he set my dad straight on what actually happened and I thereafter had to make payments to my dad for the repair bill!

I happily drove that car for quite a while, until 1970, when an electrical short under the dash burned all the wiring up while it was parked at the Clark gas station I worked at. That was the end, we had to tow it out to the junkyard. The motor was still running fine, I'm sure some racer ended up rebuilding it and had a lot of fun. Those hemi motors became very popular drag racing engines in future years.

Mom's 1961 Plymouth Valiant

Mom puts her foot down! (and on the gas pedal)
I was born in 1952. From 1957 until about 1964, my family lived in what was called "the inner core" of Milwaukee at 19th and Chambers. After marrying my dad, mom had a driver's license but never drove a car. There were plenty of bus routes near our house and many stores nearby, so my mom never felt that she had to drive, and my dad didn't want her to. I remember riding on the bus with her and there was a big Sears store within walking distance of the 19th street house.

The neighborhood we lived in was deteriorating rapidly during that time and my dad decided to look for a house in a much better area on the edge of Milwaukee's northwest side. In fact, not long after we moved, the 1960's big city race riots started all over the country and our old neighborhood was hit hard. I remember watching TV at our new house one summer night and they interrupted broadcasting, calling for all off duty firefighters and police officers in Milwaukee to report to work. My parents were sure relieved that we were away from all that!

After we moved to Lancaster Avenue, mom became increasingly frustrated by being in the "suburb" and not being able to go anywhere. There were no buses and at first we didn't even have curb, gutter and sidewalks! At that time, we had only one car, a huge pink 1957 4-door Chrysler New Yorker with a hemi engine in it.

My parents had some fierce arguments and we were not privy to all of them but dad, I'm sure, would not allow her to drive the New Yorker. No one could figure out why he was so adamant that mom not drive.

Mom had some money saved up and decided she was going to buy her own car, with or without the consent of my father. In a brilliant move, she enlisted the help of my dad's older sister, Aunt

Lorraine!

Aunt Lorraine picked up mom while dad was gone to work and they went car shopping. At the time, I had no idea of what they were up to and came home from school to find a 1961 Plymouth Valiant sitting in the driveway. It was kind of an ugly mint green 4-door. Mom spent about $300 for the car. I think Aunt Lorraine was there for moral support when dad came home the first night and helped in the ensuing confrontation. At first, dad would not allow the car to be parked in the driveway! I was about 14 or 15 years old at the time. Mom was so scared to drive the first little while, she would have me ride along with her at night while my dad was working and ask me if she was doing OK! It wasn't that long, however, before dad came to realize the benefits of mom having a car and being able to get around.

And mom helped train the Bridger boys to be some of the best drivers in the business!

My brother Russ writes: *"The reason is that it was mom who took Dan and me to the Arlen's shopping center parking lot at night so many times to practice driving, including sliding around on snow, at age 14 and 15.*

Mom had the guts and faith to trust us, and gave us her time to enable us to learn and practice. I remember in high school Driver's Education, while we students took turns driving with an instructor, he commented that I drove like an experienced driver, insinuating that I drive without a license. LOL

Mom's training and trust gave us the love of driving, and eventually the valuable careers that we all now have. Allowing us to have motorcycles at 14 also helped. Her guts to finally buy a car and get a license, disobeying dad in all his power, showed us a commitment to follow your dreams. I remember him "lobbying" against her asking us if we are ready to see her die in a car crash!

Well, mom proved him wrong and I think he grew to appreciate her new skill, grocery shopping!"

All four of us brothers now make a living driving. Our two sisters were never interested.

Years later, mom told me what she didn't know at the time: Dad considered himself (he was) an excellent driver and when younger dreamed of driving race cars. After getting married, finances were tight for so many years, he never carried liability insurance in case of an accident. That was illegal, of course, and he figured if mom started driving, the risk was much greater of an accident. I'm not sure how long it took but he did get insurance afterwards. I wonder how much trouble I would have had, being allowed to drive, if mom had not put her foot down.

Regarding that ugly green Valiant, I was less than impressed with the car when she got it. It had a 225 cu.in. slant six engine in it with a push button automatic. However, after I started reading up on it, I found that Chrysler's slant six motor had a good reputation with car guys. The engine was tilted over 30 degrees for a lower profile and extra room under the hood. It was very durable and made very good power for its size with tuned intake runners and exhaust flow. The aftermarket produced a ton of speed parts for it and I was actually getting prepared to buy some, as I thought that would be the car I would be allowed to drive after I got my driver's license.

It was all for nought, however, as I got to drive the big hemi New Yorker after my dad bought another 1957 Chrysler. It had the same 392 hemi motor in it, but it was an Imperial, Chrysler's top of the line luxury car of that year. It had leather seats, power windows and all the options. So, prior to my getting a driver's license, my dad ended up selling the Valiant, but I wasn't sorry and I loved driving that ugly pink hemi New Yorker!

My 1965 Buick GS 400

This is one of those cars I wish I would have just put away, parked in a shed for a couple of decades! I bought a really clean used 1965 Buick Gran Sport 400 convertible after I got back from active duty in the Army Reserve. This was about 1972 and I had gone through a couple of beater cars before I got my gas station. When I started to make more money, I found this car from a friend of a friend. It was in immaculate condition with not a spot of rust on it and I don't even remember what I paid for it.

Mine was a medium to dark green with a black convertible top and black interior. It had the 401 cu in V-8 with a factory 4-speed in it. It had decent power and a lot of torque for a Buick. The previous owner had installed a couple air shocks in the rear suspension that raised the back up some and firmed up the ride and handling.

It was a really nice car, but at that stage in my life, I was pretty burned out on performance cars. Before I went into the Army Reserve I had a 1962 Impala with a 300 HP 327 and factory 4-speed in it that I basically destroyed drag racing, street racing and continually breaking it. I had grown tired of the cost and hassle of constantly fixing it. The car was so bad, that my dad ended up selling it after I went on active duty for $20.00! I drove that Buick very conservatively, not wanting to break it and was very involved in getting started in business with my gas station.

The thing I remember most about that Buick is this: The engine in the car came with a Carter 4 barrel carburetor and in that model year, there was a factory option dual-quad carburetor set up. A friend of mine had another friend who just happened to have this set in his garage and was not using it at the time. We asked if we could borrow it for a couple days and put it on my engine. He agreed and we went to work after buying some new manifold gaskets. When we took it out on the street afterwards, I couldn't believe the increased power and torque the car had. It felt like a totally different vehicle and I sure wanted to keep that set-up! Unfortunately, I had to give it back.

I don't even remember what I sold that car for, but I basically gave it away. It was such a clean car and not beat up. If only I had found a place to store it. Reconditioned, it would probably be worth about $40,000 today! Oh well, just one of many of life's hard lessons and a good classic car story!

My Three Camaros, One Good,
One Bad and One Great!

1970 Camaro (The Good)

Great looking car that I bought from my friend, Tom. It was absolutely the best handling car that I have ever driven (the exception being the "Active Handling" 1999 Corvette that I had). You could almost throw that Camaro into a corner sideways, drift through it and never feel like you were out of control. Unfortunately, it was way short on power with a small 307 V-8 engine with a measly 200 HP. It would have been a fantastic car with the more powerful 350 in it, but the heavier engine might have had a negative effect on the great handling. I sure would have liked to have found out! There was an LS6 option available that year with a 450 HP 454 cubic inch monster motor in it!

1984 Camaro (The Bad)

The Camaros of the 1980's in my opinion, left a lot to be desired. The '84 I had was a well used beater that I bought and drove while saving up cash for a Corvette. If you think that '70 Camaro with a 200 HP 307 was underpowered, this had a 305 making all of 150 HP! It wasn't a bad looking car, but what a sled it was. Even brand new, I would not have liked it. Before the major redesign of the Camaro for the 1993 model year, the assembly lines were so worn out that the factory resorted to glueing some body panels together to keep them from separating after production. What probably made it worse in my mind, I owned a '93 Camaro before the '84 and was able to compare the two!

1993 Camaro (The Great!)

One of the best cars I have ever owned. I've often thought I should have kept that car, put some money into making it a supercar, instead of buying the 1999 Corvette. There were so many after-market speed parts available for them. "You never seem to know what you've had 'till it's gone!" 1993 was the first year of the completely redesigned new model. Frankly, the previous generation of the Camaro was not very good. The worn out assembly lines were so poor that Chevy resorted to gluing some of the body panels together. I started reading about a new Camaro coming out that would use the LT1 Corvette motor in the high performance Z28 version. And the Z28 would cost many thousands less than the Corvette!

Well, it took quite a few months to convince my wife that we really "needed" this car! Finally, one day I got her into a dealership to look and at least sit in the car. Immediately, she complained that she couldn't see the front of the car and she would be unable to drive it. I finally wore her down. After promising her that I would put something on the front end of the car so she would know where it is, she agreed.

Then came my wake up call! We had gone to a Chevrolet dealer in Green Bay which was a much bigger city than the small town I was living in. Although our little town of Crivitz had a Chevy dealer, I believed that I could get a better deal in the "big" city. I walked up to a salesman and asked what kind of a deal he could make me on a new Z28? His response was something to the effect that they were selling every Camaro that came in. I said "that's fine, I can special order one and wait". He then said they were getting about $2000.00 over "sticker" for them! I said something to the effect that it would be a cold day in hell before I let anyone rip me off like that! I then turned around and headed out the door.

The next day, I went in to see our small town Chevy dealer, the salesman was also a co-owner of the dealership. Knowing that they didn't have any new Camaros in stock, I walked up to him and said hello. I just stated in a matter of fact way that I wanted to buy a new Z28 Camaro, I was willing to wait to have it built and wanted to patronize a local dealer. I then stated that I knew what the invoice pricing to the dealer was and I was willing to give him $900.00 over his invoice. I almost fell over when, without even hesitating, he said "sure"! We went to his office to "spec" the car and about an hour later we had a deal. Joe Banaszak of Banaszak Chevrolet retired many years ago (the dealership has been sold), but he was a good guy to buy a car from and I'll always be grateful.

Indeed, production was behind schedule and I ended up waiting a couple months for the car. In fact, during this wait I had decided to transfer out to Utah with Ryder in July and the car still hadn't been built. The dealer worked with me and we were able to change the delivery point to Salt Lake City with another dealer doing the final setup. It was a long wait, but it was worth it. That was a great car and I kept it for 5 years and about 40,000 miles! Had a lot of fun with it and it's a great classic car story.

My 1962 Chevrolet Impala SS

All during my teenage years, I was a big fan of Chrysler products. My dad bought a used 1957 Chrysler New Yorker with a 392 cubic inch hemi motor in it, so I naturally was really into the Mopar stuff! It was the family car for several years and I kind of inherited it when I got my driver's license at 16. Unfortunately, the New Yorker was pink with a white top! But, I didn't care, that big car had a lot of torque and horsepower, it could bury that 120 MPH speedometer with no problem! It had dual exhausts on it and I bought some chrome tips to put on as well as "Hemi Powered" stickers to put on the sides. My dad was pretty amused and just shook his head!

I happily drove that car for quite a while, until a short under the dash burned all the wiring up. That was the end, we had to tow it out to the junkyard.

So, after the New Yorker died, I was seriously in need of a car, as I only had a 160cc Honda motorcycle for transportation. And my parents were certainly not going to buy me one. I had a job pumping gas at a Clark station and one of the regular customers was a young guy with a beautiful 1968 Dodge Charger RT. It had the 440 big block with a 4-speed manual and was in perfect condition. With aftermarket wheels and tires, it was a dream car. The guy treated that car like it was his baby and I never so much as saw him get on the throttle with it. One day, he told me that he could no longer afford to pay the insurance and was being forced to get rid of it. He said he would sell it to me for $1200 cash. This was in 1970 for a showroom condition '68 Charger RT! Being as I only had $400 to my name, I went home, told my dad about it and practically begged him to lend me the difference or cosign a loan. He thought about it for a bit, but told me "no". At the time I was pretty upset but looking back now, I know it was the correct answer. I would have just tore that car up and been broke all the time trying to pay the insurance.

So, a few days later, my buddy, Ross told me he had seen a nice 1962 Chevy Impala SS in a parking lot with a "For Sale" sign on it. I asked how much and he replied "$400". Exactly how much I had! Well, I wasn't a Chevy guy, but figured I'd go take a look at it. We went over and it was in great shape, had a 300HP 327 V-8 and factory 4-speed. I drove it around the block and the guy said he would take $375 for it. I went home and got my dad to come take a look at it. He looked it over and said "It's your money, buy it if you want it".

So that was the first Chevrolet that I ever owned and have had quite a few of them since! First thing I did was install glass pack mufflers, big tires and sure had a lot of fun "breaking" it. I was drag racing it out at the strip, blew the transmission twice, at least three rear ends and countless u-joints! I remember laying under that car in the back of the gas station in January. It was about 5 degrees and I was freezing my butt off putting a differential in it. Having blown it up, all I had to get back and forth to work on was my motorcycle!

By the time I went to boot camp, there wasn't much life remaining in it and my dad sold it for $20 after I left. Having blown the 4-speed twice, I couldn't afford another, so I had replaced it with a junkyard 3-speed with bad synchros in second gear. That's how I first learned to double clutch! That served me well when I later became a semi-truck driver. I could only imagine what I would have done to that Dodge Charger RT. It would have been a shame, but a good classic car story, I'm sure!

My 1967 Corvette

My fascination with Corvettes started during my pre-teen years, thanks to my Uncle Jim. My father's brother had enlisted and became a US Marine back in the late 50's. Four years later, when he got out of the service, he came home and with a bit of the cash he had saved up, bought an early 60's jet black Corvette convertible with a red interior. He drove it over to our house and it was the most beautiful car that I had ever seen! Being awestruck, I watched as he invited my dad to go for a ride with him. Of course, all Corvettes are two-seaters, so there was no room for me to go along. After they got back, he asked me if I wanted to help him wash it. Alas, I was too shy to ask and he never thought about taking me for a ride! Not too long after, he became engaged, got married and with a baby on the way, had to get rid of it. He sold it and bought a Hudson! What a letdown when I saw him in that thing!

Anyway, after that I always wanted to own a Corvette. Around 1973 or '74, I found out that a guy I went to high school with had a 1967 convertible for sale. I went over and looked at it and found it to be in decent shape. Originally, it came with a 427 cubic inch motor but the previous owner had the car stolen at some point. They recovered it a while later with the engine and transmission missing and he replaced the motor with a 327. It was a beautiful silver with a black convertible top and factory side pipes. It had the original 427 hood scoop on it and fooled a lot of people! But frankly, it wasn't much fun to drive and I put a wheelbarrow full of money into the brake system and suspension just to get it to handle properly.

In fact, returning from a vacation trip to Canada, I had a rear wheel come off on me while driving down the highway near Oconto, Wisconsin. The break down was due to a mechanic previously improperly tightening an axle retaining nut. Fortunately, the wheel came off and wedged up in the wheel well, so there was no body damage. Earlier that same day, I had received a speeding ticket from a Michigan State Trooper in the Upper Peninsula! The repair bill was about $250.00 and I had to pay for a motel overnight while the mechanic waited for parts. The following day I got home with only a couple dollars left in my wallet. That was a rather lousy trip home.

It wasn't long before I grew tired of the ongoing expense and put it up for sale. I paid $2500 for it and sold it for the same amount. Wouldn't you know it, not long after, the prices on used Corvettes and muscle cars started to skyrocket? In fact, the guy I bought it from called me back a few months later and wanted to buy it back from me, if I still had it. The numbers didn't match, because of the replacement engine and transmission, but I'm sure I would have gotten a lot more for it, had I kept it another year!

My 1976 Ford F-250 Highboy

Throughout the 1970's I had a Clark gas station in Milwaukee with a large lot that needed snow plowing in the Wisconsin winters. I decided to buy a vehicle with a plow in order to do my own lot as well as start a side business plowing snow for others. After buying a used early 1970's Bronco, and using it for a couple years, I was not very happy with it. It had a 6 cylinder engine with automatic transmission and I was afraid it was not built to stand up to commercial snow plowing use.

I talked to my dad and he agreed to finance me on purchasing a new pickup. Being partial to the F-250 as my buddy had a 1974 model, I visited a Ford dealer in Milwaukee to see what a new one would cost. The salesman proceeded to try and "empty my wallet" and I got so mad that I walked out of the dealership. The next day I drove about 40 miles away to West Bend where they had another Ford dealer, warning the salesman of my bad experience in Milwaukee the day before.

Being forewarned he came up with what I thought was a pretty fair deal. I ordered a new black Ranger XLT with just about every option checked on the form including heavy duty 7800LB GVWR, dual batteries, high output alternator, A/C, manual tranny and lockout hubs. The total price was right about $8,000 and adding a Western 4-way snowplow was an additional $1,200. It was a standard cab with the eight foot bed, chrome tie-downs and marker lights, a great looking truck. Having to wait a few weeks for delivery, I was pretty excited, taking delivery of my 1976 model in December of 1975. That is my truck on the right in the photo at a friend's hunting cabin, the only one I could find.

That turned out to be a hell of a truck that I kept for 16 years until I moved to Utah in 1993. It let me down only one time with dead batteries in all those years. Although it rode like a cement truck when I got it due to the optional heavy duty suspension, I was able to mellow it out a little by removing three leaves from the rear springs on each side. 1976 was the last model year for the 360 V-8 engine, they went to a 400 V-8 the following year. The truck felt somewhat underpowered when I got it so I took off the tiny two barrel carburetor and replaced it with a Holley 500cfm two barrel. I didn't even have to change the manifold. That, along with putting a dual exhaust system on it made a huge improvement and I was really happy with it. Except for the mileage, which was 10 MPG loaded or empty, but fortunately, I had a gas station. One of the option boxes I should have checked was for an auxiliary fuel tank!

That truck was a snow plowing machine and I never had trouble going through anything. I kept the standard size mud and snow tires on it for plowing and some big 32 inch road tires and wheels on for the summer. After I put over 30 thousand miles on, it turned out the 360 had an inherent oiling problem in the crankcase. A rod started knocking and I took it back to the Ford dealer in West Bend(I was actually able to drive it out there). Thankfully they covered it under an extended factory warranty, pulled the motor, completely rebuilt it and I never had another problem with that truck. I think I put about 150,000 miles on it before I left Wisconsin.

My 1971 Honda CB750 (811cc)!

After becoming a franchised gasoline dealer in the early 1970's, I started to make a little money. After selling the Honda CB160 I bought from my dad it was time for another motorcycle, a big one. My dad was by then riding a 450 cc Honda. The biggest Honda they made at that time was the 4 cylinder, 4 carburetor 750 cc and I started looking for a good used one. An older guy had a 1971 for sale with low miles that was in excellent condition. It was dark green and the owner had put saddlebags on it along with a windshield. He was longing for a Harley Davidson for him and his wife, so he made me a pretty good deal on it for $1400. Of course, the first thing I did was to take the bags and windshield off, as I wanted a performance bike!

And it sure was fast, compared to anything else that I had ridden. My buddy, Ross had recently purchased a new Harley Sportster and all he could do was eat my dust at every traffic light. I rode that bike for a year or so and had a lot of fun with it. One day, I got on the throttle hard and the chain broke, bunching up and punching a hole in the aluminum crankcase. "Damn", I knew this was going to be an expensive repair and boy, was I right. A new crankcase alone was over $200 and the quote from the dealer to take the engine out, tear down and rebuild it was ridiculous. So, after buying a shop manual, I decided to remove the motor myself and let the dealer do the engine work. It was a big job to pull that motor but wasn't too difficult with the step by step instruction provided in the book. During the time spent doing that, I figured, if I'm going to spend all this money on it, I want a better bike after it is done. So, after getting some performance ideas from the dealer, I had them bore the block out to 811 cc and put a hot cam in it. After getting the engine back in the bike, I re-jetted the carburetors and put a low restriction exhaust on it. And what a world of difference in the performance! I don't remember what the total cost ended up being (it wasn't cheap), but I was sure happy with it.

I took it out to the drag strip and was running mid-twelve second quarter miles with it at over 103 MPH. That was a pretty fast motorcycle back in the 1970's! That was a fun bike to ride and I sold it just before I got married to my first wife about 1975. Having sold it to the brother of a friend, I kept track of it and actually tried to buy the bike back in the mid-80's after the guy had stopped riding it, due to a serious work injury. The bike had been sitting outdoors for a couple years and it would have been way too much work to get it back in running condition. So, I passed on it and bought a really nice 1983 Honda V65 Magna. But, that's another story.

My 1983 Honda V65 Magna

After selling my 1971 Honda 750 back in Milwaukee in the mid 70's, I went for quite a few years without owning a motorcycle. In 1981, I moved north to Crivitz, Wi and a few years later started getting the urge for another bike.

I knew the guy I sold the 750 to, he was the brother of a good friend in Milwaukee, and I knew he still had the bike. I was aware that he had been injured seriously in an industrial accident and was no longer able to ride. My first thought was to contact him through my friend Ross and see if he was interested in selling it back to me and he was. When I owned it, I had the engine bored out to 811 cc and installed a hot cam in it. It was a good bike with a lot of power (it would run 12 second quarter miles) and thought I'd have fun restoring it. But after making a trip down to Milwaukee with a trailer and seeing it, I quickly changed my mind. The bike had been sitting outdoors for a couple years and was in very bad shape. The carburetors had been removed and they were just laying there on the engine, the intakes to the combustion chambers wide open. The tires and seat upholstery were just completely rotted out. So I said "thanks, but no thanks", left it and returned home.

This was about 1985 and I started looking in the paper for a used bike, coming across an ad for a '83 V65 Magna. I knew it was a big bike with an 1100 cc motor in it, but not much else. I really had not been paying much attention to the newer motorcycles that had been coming out. This bike happened to be in Milwaukee, so I made the 300 mile round trip back down there the following weekend to look at it. It was black, good looking and appeared to be in very good condition. The guy wanted $2200 for it so I made the deal, rode it back to Crivitz while my wife drove the car back. It was a very cold, windy day in March with the temperature barely above 40 degrees, a very "chilly" 150 mile Wisconsin ride!

After getting it home, licensed and registered, I had to wait to get some decent riding weather. While taking it for a test ride before buying, I knew it was a fast bike but didn't know how fast! The long ride home was cold and miserable and I really didn't open it up. Waiting for decent weather, I started reading a few road tests and discovered what a powerful machine I had just purchased. Once the weather cleared, getting that thing out on the street and cranking it up, I couldn't believe how fast the bike was. It had well over 100 horsepower, with a ten thousand RPM redline on the tach! It could run the quarter mile in ten seconds and quickly found that you better have a firm grip on the handlebars when you opened up the throttle! The acceleration was just phenomenal and something I will never forget! I remember some of the yells, comments (and a few screams!) while giving people rides! It would be getting close to 90 MPH in third gear, with three more gears available! I sure had fun with it, keeping it about two years before buying a new '87 Goldwing Interstate. The Goldwing turned out to be a mistake, as I really missed the performance and handling of the Magna after I sold it. The Goldwing was just too big and heavy, although it did have a good ride.

My First Florida Car - 1973 Buick Century

While living in Wisconsin back in the 1980's, I was able to purchase two Florida cars thanks to my dad. He retired from Chrysler in Milwaukee after working there for 30 years. He was only 52 years old in 1979, sold their house and moved the family to Sarasota, Florida. My three youngest siblings moved with my parents as they were still in school. I was already 27 years old and on my own, remaining in Milwaukee.

One day, it was about 1980, I got a call from my dad. He said he had a neighbor across the street that was getting too old to drive and wanted to sell his car. It was a 1973 Buick Century with V-8 and automatic that only had about 12,000 miles on it. Yellow with a black top, he said it still looked brand new and was willing to sell it for $2,000.00. I said "hell yes" and started calling for a plane ticket and to arrange for a few days off.

I flew down a few days later and we went across the street and made the deal. The guy had a car port with no garage and I asked if I could keep it parked there until I left and he said "sure". It rained overnight and the next morning we were outside and he came out with a towel to give me. I asked what it was for and he said that he always wiped the car down after a rain to keep it looking good. I was young, kind of stupid yet, and was about to say that was not going to happen when I got the car back to Wisconsin. My dad must have sensed this as he took the towel, handed it to me and I got the hint that I'd better do it, LOL.

That was a good car that I had for over 10 years and put well over 100,000 miles on it. With a 350 cu. in. V-8 and a two barrel carburator, it had decent power but a four barrel would have really made it go. I thought about replacing the carb but just never got around to it.

With only 12,000 miles on it I'm sure the car had the original tires on that were by that time seven years old. It handled kind of crappy on the highway when I drove it back to Wisconsin so I put a set of (one size over) Michelin tires on with four heavy duty Monroe shocks. After putting a smaller aftermarket steering wheel on, it drove like a freak'in sports car. I was pretty happy with it.

As I happily found out, after buying a second Florida car thanks to my dad, older retirement areas are prime spots to find deals on used vehicles, including motorhomes. It only makes sense, as a lot of them age out or die off and their vehicles need to be sold. Older people of means tend to maintain and not abuse their stuff. It certainly helps to have family or friends in the area to watch for deals.

My Second Florida Car - 1983 Buick Regal Limited

In 1980, my dad found me a great deal on a used 1973 Buick Century that I happily drove more than 100,000 miles with no problems. About 1988, he called again, perfect timing as the old '73 Century was starting to wear out. This time, he knew an elderly man who lived about a block away and decided to sell his car. It was a fully loaded 1983 Buick Regal Limited with 8,000 miles on it!

The guy bought it new when he was 90 years old and drove it for 5 years before he got into a fairly minor traffic accident that damaged the front end. A body shop had fixed the damage and it looked and drove like a brand new car. That crash convinced him to give up driving and he wanted to get rid of it. With only 8,000 miles in 5 years he sure didn't use the car much and it was always kept in a garage.

Like I stated, the car was loaded with a V-6 motor, padded vinyl top, fancy wheels and power everything. It felt like a very luxurious car driving it. The factory sticker was still in the glove box, with the MSRP at $13,500. That was not inexpensive for a car in 1983. My dad had driven it, said it was good and I told him to make the deal and I'll find a way to get down there.

That also was a great car right up until early 1993 when I started hearing lifter noise whith the engine fully warmed up. I had always religiously maintained that car and was very surprised it let me down. This happened just as I was getting ready to make the move to Salt Lake City in July. Being just about ready to load up a U-haul truck, I got a trailer to haul my other car and decided the leave the Regal behind. My wife had to stay an extra month to close on the house so she drove it until then, took it to a used car lot in Crivitz and took whatever the owner would give us. The amount he offered was ridiculously low, so I had not one pang of guilt selling the car to him. In fact, I believe he could have replaced the motor and still have made money reselling it.

My Ride Along - Richard Petty Driving Experience

Looking forward to watching the Daytona 500 got me thinking about a ride-along I went on at the Las Vegas Motor Speedway back in the early 2000's. At the time I had a 1999 Corvette C5 and drove down to Vegas From Salt Lake City for a few days on a mini-vacation. It was in March and the weather was getting to be ideal in Las Vegas. I had been reading about the "Richard Petty Driving Experience" being put on at various race tracks throughout the country and one of the tracks was at the Vegas Speedway. They hold a NASCAR race every year in spring.

As stated at the Petty website: "Roll the dice in Las Vegas and feel the adrenaline rush behind the wheel of a 600 HP NASCAR race car. The nightlife on the Las Vegas Strip may be legendary, but when the sun is up the action is always at Las Vegas Motor Speedway's top attraction, Richard Petty Driving Experience. There is no better way to complete your trip to Las Vegas than to challenge your friends and family on the track at speeds of up to 155 MPH."

They offer various packages, depending on your budget and appetite for adventure. Various options include a three lap ride-along with a professional driver or "drive it yourself" deals. You can go through a class and drive a car for eight laps starting at $500 all the way up to 50 laps for about $2700! You actually drive a car similar to the ones they use in the Nationwide Series (about 600 HP), not the more powerful Sprint Cup cars. If you do the eight lap "drive it yourself" package, they do not just turn you loose on the track and run 'till you crash. You have to follow behind a real race driver who will get you up to some serious speed but he will not let you run wild out there. You can understand that for $500, they don't want you crashing their car!

Before we made the trip down there, I did a lot of research, at first thinking seriously that I wanted to drive one of these cars. After considering all the options, I figured that if I really wanted to witness the power of these cars and really get a feel of what it's like going all out in a real race car, the ride-along would be the best option. I would have liked to do both, but it was too pricey for me. Back then you could do the ride along for about $100, it's more like $175 now.

So after deciding what I wanted, we drove out to the speedway the next morning. It was a clear, cool day with the temperature only in the 50's, but perfect for being inside a race car! We got to watch for a while as the customers who were paying to drive were going through their training class and getting fitted with race suits. They would take them out in small groups of 4 or 5 at a time. In between, the professional drivers would take the ride along customers out. The cars had a passenger seat in them with full restraints, same as the driver. Ride-alongs were not required to wear a racing suit, but they did furnish you with a helmet. The ride would consist of three "hot laps" with two professional drivers, each with a passenger, going full speed and "racing" together. Of course, they would not do anything stupid trying to beat each other but they did really did duel.

I began to worry about how dumb I would look trying to climb into the car, as there were no doors on it and you had to go in through the window. Actually, it wasn't bad, as I was able to get a firm grip on the roll bar to help boost myself in. As soon as we (me and the passenger in the other car) were buckled in, a photographer came over and took photos, which we had the option of purchasing after the ride.

After he jumped back over the wall and got strapped in, my driver asked "are you ready for some serious speed?" As the signal was given to go I replied "I sure am!". We followed the other car out of the pit and my driver floored the throttle in first gear. I couldn't believe the push back in the seat I felt as the car surged ahead. It seemed like a long time before he shifted into second gear as the motor must have a redline on the tach in the 10,000 RPM range (I couldn't see the tach). As he hit second gear and then third through the first corner and into the second, fourth as we came around onto the back straight, we seemed to be flying with the same push back in the seat, but we were still not up to full speed. On the straight we were up alongside the other car and probably doing better than 160 MPH as corner three was coming up. As we got closer and closer, every instinct in my body was telling me we were going way too fast and would never make it through the corner! I must have had a death grip on whatever I could hang on to. However, I had failed to take into account the severe 20 degree banking on the track that allows the cars to corner at much higher speeds! Once into the corner, and realizing that we weren't going to crash, I was amazed as I could feel the car in a gentle 4 wheel drift as my driver used the throttle to control the car. It was almost as if you were sliding around a corner in snow, using the throttle and steering to control your drift. Only, we were going 150 something miles per hour! And we were racing right alongside the other guy! So for three laps we were dicing back and forth and it was one of the most thrilling things I have ever experienced! I tell you what, after getting done and leaving the track, my Corvette felt kind of slow!

Bottom line, I would recommend a ride-along to anyone who is a NASCAR fan. While watching NASCAR on TV now, I still remember the feeling of going through those corners on the track. It's something you will never forget! A friend of mine actually did the "drive it yourself" 8 lap deal a couple years ago and had a blast also. You can do whatever suits you, someday I would like to go back and do the driving.

Going Back to Drive - Richard Petty Driving Experience

A couple years back I went for a ride-along with the Richard Petty Driving Experience at the Las Vegas Motor Speedway in the early 2000's. I had a blast as my driver dueled back and forth with another race driver and his passenger for three laps around the 1.5 mile speedway. I've wanted to go back and try driving myself ever since, and it has been one of a couple things in my "bucket list" to do before I get too old and feeble. Now at 62 years of age, I thought I'd better get to it as my wife and I planned a week-long vacation in Vegas. I invited my buddy and his wife to fly down from Wisconsin and meet us and they said "sure". They're already retired, it must be nice!

In March of 2014 I found a 10 percent off deal on the internet for the Petty Experience. I scheduled a ride-along at 10:30am for my wife Mary and the 8 lap driving experience for me at 12 noon. The prices had not changed much from the previous visit, ride-alongs a little over $100 and the 8 lap rookie driving event a little over $400.

MARY'S RIDE-ALONG

We arrived at the track on a Tuesday at 10am and got my wife signed up. Things have changed up a little from when I did it. In those days the passengers were just given a helmet and nothing else. Now, you have to get in a race suit with a helmet that is miked up with an audio/video connection. They record your entire ride with a camera on the passenger that also looks forward out the windshield. You can buy the video for an extra $50.

Instead of two cars going side by side for three laps, Mary and her driver went out alone. They only sent out one car at a time and I noticed that they used a different set of cars for the ride-alongs. The professional drivers use cars that aren't rev limited like the other set they let the rookies drive. They all have about 600 horsepower and the ride-along cars will do better than 160 MPH. I remember from my old ride that my driver could actually drift his car in the corners a bit pretty effortlessly. The rookie driving cars are rev limited to about 140 MPH. Mary had a blast and after getting out of the car, said she wished that they could have kept going for a while.

MY DRIVE

Upon our arrival, they told me to be at the driver's meeting room at 11:30am for my scheduled noon drive. I went in and got my paperwork taken care of and sat down to wait. Soon they fitted us with racing suits and then got us into a room where we watched some videos while they prepared the track. Our crew chief for the program came in and talked us through a video of the track, giving us information to be aware of during our drive.

After that was done we walked out to the pit area to be fitted with helmets before our turn came up. They had us on a list and would call us up to get ready as other drivers finished. The helmets were equipped with two way microphones so the instructor could talk to you while in the car. They also had the audio-video connection to record your drive, which you could purchase for another $100.

When my turn came up the crew chief escorted me over the wall to the car. I noticed climbing in through the window that the seats seemed to be even more restrictive than before. It took some effort to get my butt into the bucket and squeeze my helmeted head through the window at the same time (also due to the fact of being more than a few pounds heavier since the last time), but once I was in it was comfortable. They attach the back of your helmet to the seat back and it is impossible to turn your head much at all. In the picture of me in the driver's seat, that was as far as I could turn my head.

The instructor introduced himself and pictures were taken. After last minute instructions he asked if I was ready to go and I said yes. The differential is geared low for the high speeds on the track so you have to give it some throttle as you let out the clutch. I managed to get going without stalling it and the power and sound of it was thrilling as I gave it about half throttle and shifted to second gear. The instructor was talking and guiding me out the exit lane and told me when to get up onto the track. The first lap was to get the feel of the track and I steadily gave it more throttle and got up to speed. I remembered the steep banking from my ride-along so I was not surprised by it. They had a single orange cone just past the pits going into the first corner where you were instructed to lift off the throttle for a bit until you got to a second pair of orange cones where you got back on it at full throttle.

After completing the first lap my instructor told me to go ahead and crank it up. At the double cones I mashed the throttle as we were up in the banking and the car took off. I was pretty nervous the first few laps and tended to lift a bit approaching the corners, but my lap times improved by more than one second on each successive lap as I got more comfortable with the car. The car's suspension is set up for the steep banking and it was somewhat difficult to make a smooth transition onto the back straight, as the car wants to keep turning left and you have to really fight the wheel to keep it going straight. I was surprised at the force needed but as soon as the car got back into the banking it naturally wanted to go with it and was comfortable to drive.

I knew from pre-race instruction and my own experience that you have to look far ahead down the track when you're going that fast to stay in a good line. They did have markers painted at various points on the track to aim for. Still, I almost immediately became disoriented as to where we were on the track, and only knew that we went past the pit area when I passed the single orange cone where you lift on the throttle. You just don't have time to look at anything except the track ahead of you. You're listening for any word the instructor says, if he doesn't say anything, the crew chief told us that is good. I was glad my guy was pretty quiet. On one corner he corrected my line by reaching over and turning the wheel slightly left, as he told me to stay a little further off the wall. There was one recurring corner where the sun was in my eyes making it difficult to see through it and was nerve wracking to me. I had my regular darkening transition lens glasses on and sure wished I would have brought my prescription sunglasses.

It was a great experience that I will always remember, some day maybe I'll do it again. Richard Petty runs a great program, I would only suggest one thing. While they show you a video in the meeting room of the track and talk you through it, I wish they would have taken us out in a couple of vans for a couple laps to get a better feel of the layout. Other than that minor point, I had a blast and have a much better understanding of the physical effort and concentration it takes to drive one of these cars fast. I would have been totally exhausted within a short period of time, had they let me continue on. Oh, how I wish they would have let me! If you decide to try it, don't forget your sunglasses!

Why I Absolutely Hate Buying Cars!

I've always been a car guy and have been fortunate to have owned some great ones in my life. The buying process for me, however, has always been stressful and it sucks. Although I've managed to get some fantastic deals on some awesome cars, I've also been ripped off, mostly when I was a much younger man, and those memories are not pleasant.

Back in 2015, my old beater work car (1999 Dodge Neon) seemed to be about ready to expire so I started looking for a replacement. Wanting to buy something reliable as a second car to get back & forth to work that would last a few years until retirement, I searched the online private seller ads for a decent vehicle. I came across an ad for a 2006 PT Cruiser convertible with a turbo that had only 50,000 miles on it.

Owned by a retired couple who towed it down to Arizona every winter behind their RV. Great looking car with good paint and like-new top. The price was right about book value. This is gotta be good, right?. Didn't do any other research, raced over, did a quick test drive, and plunked the money down. What a piece of crap that car turned out to be. It was a money pit that I couldn't trust to even start after 2 tows to a dealer. I finally got fed up, decided to absorb a huge loss, and bite the bullet. I put the car in a local online ad Tuesday, trying to get a decent price for it, went out to clean it, retracted the top for the first time this year and the rear window wouldn't go down. Come on! Another trip to the dealer? That was my breaking point.

In April of 2017, I went online to search vehicle inventories at nearby dealers. I've spent a lot of time researching cars the last few weeks and found a 2016 Nissan Altima at a dealer only a couple miles away from me. I rented a 2016 Altima to drive back to Wisconsin the previous September (didn't trust the PT Cruiser) and was very impressed with the roomy, comfortable car, great power and 38 MPG average on the round trip.

This car was one of the dealer's own fleet vehicles, well equipped and had only 8,000 miles on it (some were most likely rental miles). It was first titled in July of 2016. The ad said it was a "Certified Used Car" with extended warranty, so I took the PT Cruiser over to see what they would give me for it, knowing it wouldn't be much. To make a long story a little shorter, we went back and forth, me taking another $2000 hit on the trade-in, but the Altima was well more than $2000 under book. I'm thinking, go for it and get this POS Chrysler off my back....

Then the game begins: The price of $15,000 for the Altima was only good if I financed it through Nissan. It amazes me that they don't even want your cash anymore. They make a commission from Nissan finance based on as much as they can lend for as long a period as possible, assuming they can qualify you. OK, for that price, I'm thinking I can pay it off or refi in a couple months.

I specifically remember the exact words of the salesman when looking at the car, " This is a 'certified used car' and comes with a 7 year, 100,000 mile warranty in addition to the three year factory warranty". The salesman then had me at a table, another guy hanging out within earshot. We worked the numbers and I asked what other fees they would come up with. I specifically remember again the exact words, "document prep fee of $295, taxes, registration and license fees". The other guy hanging out would jump in, coaching up the salesman(boy) after I asked questions. I agreed to make the deal. I then sat and twiddled my thumbs for 45 minutes while they "did the paperwork". Meanwhile, they take the license plates off my PT Cruiser and inform me that they're in the trunk of my "new car". Finally the finance dude calls me in to start signing papers.

He's shoving papers in front of me to sign like I'm buying a freakin house, telling me I'm getting the first three oil changes and inspections at no charge. Paper after paper, no contract, I was getting a bad feeling this was not going to turn out well. Of course, the second last document was "the contract", and that contract was about $3000.00 more than what we agreed to! Those first 3 oil changes? That was going to cost me a $100 maintenance fee. That 7 year, 100,00 mile warranty? It was $2000.00 extra. Line item "Gap" charge $895.00? I asked "what the hell is that?". Answer: "That is Gap insurance, in case you total the car and you are upside down on your payments". Emissions and safety inspection? $100.00. Double the price you'd pay at a regular emission site.

My then 64 year old temper erupted. Without detailing the entire conversation, suffice to say a few bad words in a very irate voice were said by me, a gal that was busy photocopying, put down her papers and abruptly left the room. I told him "put the license plates back on my PT Cruiser, I'll find somewhere else to buy a car". As I started to get up, he got his hands up in the air saying "hold on, hold on, let me fix this".

He had to tear up the contract and write a new one as well as redo the finance agreement, and he was not happy, desperately pleading non-stop that I absolutely "needed" that $2000 extended warranty. I told him that they should have been upfront with me at the beginning, I was not going to be played for a fool and I'm not paying for an additional warranty. After signing the revisions, he walked out of his office saying he would find my salesman. The prick never even said thanks or goodbye, leaving me standing there. He had the temporary registration tag for the back window in his hand and stuck it on the showroom door as he went outside while calling the salesman on a two-way radio. He never came back, the photocopy gal was gone, as well as a couple other people that had been standing around outside his open office door. The salesman came and got me after a couple minutes.That's supposed to make me feel guilty? Think I would recommend them to anyone else? Hell no! I'm hoping Nissan contacts me for a review of my "car buying" experience.

You have to be prepared to stand your ground and remember what is stated, they will clean your pockets for everything they can get! One thing I learned over these many years, think clearly and be prepared to walk away from a bad deal. And doing some research would have saved me a bunch of wasted money on that PT Cruiser, a lesson I should have remembered! Consumer Reports has vast data on the reliability history of automobiles. If you're in the market for a vehicle, you can pay $6.95 per month for a few months while you do your homework. Edmunds.com is a pretty good source that is also free.

Hopefully, if I have to buy another vehicle in my life, there will be a better way to do it, or in my old age, I may throw my future cane or walker at the next guy.

A Pleasant Car Buying Experience?
What a Surprise!

Back in April of 2017 I ranted and raved over the poor treatment I received from a Nissan dealer in Taylorsville, Utah during the process of buying a 2016 Nissan
Altima.

I thought it only fair to acknowledge an extremely pleasant experience in the purchase of a new Ford Escape in 2019.

LuAnn's 2009 Escape, purchased new, had over 210,000 miles on it and she decided it was time for a new vehicle. It had been a great car with 4WD that never gave her any trouble so we started researching the 2019 models. Because there is a new redesign coming in the 2020 Escape going on sale this fall, Ford has some large cash incentives probably, I was thinking, to reduce the 2019 inventory.

We stopped over to Witt Ford in Crivitz on a Sunday to look over the lot, went back on Tuesday to test drive the one and really liked it. It was well equipped and not loaded up with all the extra features and cost she didn't need or want. Based on previous experience, going inside to talk about price, I was not looking forward to doing battle with a sales team again.

The same salesman, Robin, was there from whom LuAnn bought her last car 10 years prior and we went to his office. There basically was nothing to haggle over as his first offer had a substantial discount from the MSRP and all the available incentives from Ford were included. That reduced the sticker price by about 22 percent. LuAnn agreed to the figures and we made an appointment to pick up the car the next day.

Next afternoon, we came back, and it was time to meet Dan, the "finance guy", to sign the paperwork. That was my "here we go to battle" time that I dreaded, remembering my last experience in Salt Lake City. We went in, sat down, looked over the contract. All the numbers were what was agreed to with no "surprises" added on. He showed us a sheet describing various extras like extended warranty, finish protection, etc that we could add but there was no hard sell and no objection over declining!

This is one of only two car buying experiences in my life that were actually pleasant and I have bought quite a few cars over the last 50 plus years. And, amazingly, the other great one was also here in Crivitz way back in 1993 at Banaszak Chevrolet. That dealership changed hands many years ago and is now owned by someone else that I have not had any experience with. For a great many years I was always under the impression I could get a better deal from the "big city" dealers but my opinion has certainly changed!

As Ernie Von Schledorn would say "Who do you know wants to buy a car?", I would add "in Crivitz?" Ernie was a German immigrant car dealer in Milwaukee for over 50 years with that famous slogan.

Mike Kauffman Photo
Ryder Integrated Logistics Tractor pulling Swire
Coca-Cola trailer based in Salt Lake City, Ut

ACKNOWLEDGEMENT

Paperback book cover photo credit: Mike Kauffman
**Ryder Integrated Logistics tractor pulling
Swire Coca Cola trailer.**

Photo Credit: Mike Kauffman

Photo Credit: Mike Kauffman

ABOUT THE AUTHOR

Daniel S Bridger

Retired as of January, 2018. I have spent 37 years (24 as a trainer) driving tractor-trailer combinations and being involved in 3rd party logistics. Experienced in driver hiring, recruiting, training, safety and DOT compliance.
Certified Smith System Driver instructor.

Printed in Great Britain
by Amazon

49291393R00071